SELECTED SERMONS OF
THOMAS AQUINAS MCGOVERN, S.J.

Selected Sermons of Thomas Aquinas McGovern, s.j.

Feasts & Seasons of the Liturgical Year

Edited by Suzie Andres
Foreword by Dr. Ronald P. McArthur

Thomas Aquinas College
Santa Paula, California

The image of the sunburst on the cover and throughout this book was inspired by an inlaid marble version in the rotunda of St. Thomas Hall on the Thomas Aquinas College campus. The symbol of the school's patron, the sunburst recalls the description of St. Thomas by Pope Leo XIII in his encyclical *Aeterni Patris*:

> Among the Scholastic Doctors, the chief and master of all towers Thomas Aquinas, who … is rightly and deservedly esteemed the special bulwark and glory of the Catholic faith. With his spirit at once humble and swift, his memory ready and tenacious, his life spotless throughout, a lover of truth for its own sake, richly endowed with human and divine science, like the sun he heated the world with the warmth of his virtues and filled it with the splendor of his teaching.

"IHS" is an ancient monogram of the name of Jesus Christ which became popular as a symbol (often surrounded by rays) toward the close of the Middle Ages. In the sixteenth century, St. Ignatius of Loyola adopted the monogram in his seal as general of the Society of Jesus, and thus it became the emblem of his institute.

Cover art, cover design, and interior design by Cara Peden

For Marilyn McArthur & Cathy Walsh

I will give you treasures out of the darkness,
And riches that have been hidden away,
That you may know that I am the Lord,
The God of Israel, who calls you by your name.

— Isaiah 45:3

CONTENTS

LENT

HOLY WEEK

EASTER

II. FEASTS AND OCCASIONS

FOREWORD

Knowing he was dying, but having long desired to see the publication of these sermons, Dr. McArthur dictated this foreword at his home the week before he passed away.

I first came across Reverend Thomas Aquinas McGovern, S.J., in reading parts of his doctoral thesis. I didn't know who he was then, and I thought as I read, "This is really, really good." He worked very hard on it, and it turned out that was true of him: everything he did he worked hard on. He wouldn't play tennis if he had to give a sermon, and his duties were always first. Yet he did like to relax; he wasn't any Gradgrind.

Having studied at Laval, he was a disciple of St. Thomas and Aristotle. He found people of like mind at the College. He contacted us when we were up and running in Calabasas.

You pick up things about character that register with you, that make a tremendous impression on you. It just happens in conversation; it's inadvertent, but makes its impact. At his job interview we loved him; we wanted him with us. He said, "I'll have to change; I'll have to do something I've never done before. I'll have to do seminar mode" — and we thought he could. He had been used to lecturing back at Canisius. The most extraordinary thing about Father was that he did make the transition; he changed his whole mode of teaching and became a superior tutor in this program.

He first lived in the dormitories, but he couldn't stand the noise. So he went over and lived in the basement in the Hacienda — it was really primitive — where he carved out a room: a bed, a nightstand, a desk. He used to say to me, "It's quiet here; I can study."

He studied very, very hard. For every class he prepared as thoroughly as he could prepare it given the time he had — *every* class. He was truly remarkable, Thomas Aquinas McGovern.

We were lucky to have him. Up until that time, and maybe afterwards, I would prepare classes just in order to get through the material in time, to cover the content. That was not sufficient for him. He wanted to be able to understand, and if students raised difficulties in the classes, he would take those difficulties very seriously. I learned from him the importance of preparing as well as I could the things I was teaching, not to slough them off. You can know a lot more than the students and get through the day, but that wasn't good enough for him. He had to try to understand, he had to be there with the students in the different parts of what he was teaching, to be there intellectually with the students.

He was known for being thorough and for giving no cheap answers to any questions. He would much rather say, "I don't know how to answer," than try to look good. He liked the students that worked hard and were there for the right reasons. He asked questions, probed, didn't give easy answers. He made them think. He was really successful with students, and his reputation grew quickly. He's a legend around the school now.

He always thought I was more intelligent than he, and knew more. He would come to me to discuss questions, and a day later he would come back and say, "Thanks for helping me; that was such a big help. I truly appreciate your taking the time and care with me."

He loved sports, American male sports, football. St. Mary's had a famous annual game with Fordham back in New York, and he knew all about the games, had newspaper clips from all of them; and at the same time he had no use for people who didn't study. So he wasn't a man whose attention was fixed on athletics — much more important for him was learning.

We went down once to a tennis tournament on the way to San Diego. We watched the greatest tennis players of the day, and his reaction was, "I had no idea of the intricacies of tennis, but after Ron explained things to me, I could see more and more." He had no sense of superiority, no urge to be known.

Fr. McGovern never aimed to be a chaplain. His interest lay in teaching and learning. When we wanted him to be on the Board of Governors of the school, he didn't want to do that; he didn't want anybody to pay attention to him at all.

He was not effeminate in any way. He was a man's man, and yet he had a very nice way with women; with the girl students, he was courteous, friendly. He had sisters, and it showed in his ways. He was a tremendous man, very serious. Yet at the same time, he had a light touch and a dry, dry sense of humor. I don't think you could ever feel oppressed by him, that he had designs on you or knew what you should do or be; he just wanted the students to develop and learn things.

You always saw Fr. McGovern in the habit. Once a year he would have his provincial come out to the College and check what he was doing; he was subject to his provincial. I think he loved being a Jesuit. He stayed true to that formation.

After he died, when we went back with his body to Fordham, a lot of the Jesuits I met there knew him. They had gone through school with him, and they said about him, "He always obeyed the Rule, never shaving it, never knowing better than others how to train Jesuits." They had a kind of admiration about that. His view was if some situation was doing harm to your soul, then exit it. He remained a good Jesuit, but lived without the benefit of his community.

The main thing I learned from Fr. McGovern is to put your heart and soul into what you are doing and really do it as well as you can — not as well as someone else can do it, but as well as *you* can. That's a tremendous lesson.

His Sermons

I think his are the best sermons you can read now. I can't believe that Chrysostom and the Fathers of the Church have written better; his sermon on the Blessed Sacrament, in particular, is simply breathtaking.

Fr. McGovern prepared for his sermons the same as he prepared for class: thoroughly. He would go to St. Thomas almost exclusively, and this resulted in sermons which reached the center of the matter at hand.

He came to the College because he thought he could learn more here than any other place. You see in at least some of these sermons that he was learning things as he wrote them.

He delivered these sermons very seriously, as something into which he had poured his heart and soul; they were, as you can see, well thought out. In them Fr. McGovern sought to teach, and in teaching, to feed our inborn hunger to know God so that we could draw ever closer to Him Who is our reason for being.

Ronald P. McArthur
Santa Paula
October 15, 2013
Feast of St. Teresa of Avila

EDITOR'S NOTES

1. Father McGovern did not date his sermons. I estimate that the earliest included here is from about 1965, and that he prepared and preached the majority at Thomas Aquinas College between 1972 and 1985.

2. Father occasionally named his sermons (for example, "Cana") or identified the cycle of liturgical readings on which he was preaching. I have kept his titles and included the year (A, B, or C) when applicable.

3. Footnotes identify Father's references to Scripture. For sermons in which he preached primarily on the Scriptures, key references are under the sermon's title; in the interest of simplicity, these are not repeated in the footnotes. As to translations, Father used, among others, the Douay-Rheims, Revised Standard Version, Knox, New American, and sometimes his own.

4. "Secunda Secundae" refers to the Second Part of the Second Part of St. Thomas Aquinas' *Summa Theologiae*; "Tertia Pars" refers to the Third Part of the *Summa*.

5. I have added footnotes for references to St. Thomas when they are not complete in the sermon. Where quotations from the Church Fathers come through St. Thomas, one reference supplies for all.

6. Father McGovern used to quip, "If you preach for more than ten minutes, you cease to be appreciated." True, perhaps, but I have added a second sermon for those Sundays and Feasts on which his thoughtful brevity leaves us longing for more and his due diligence provided for just such an exigency.

I

Seasons of the Liturgical Year

ADVENT

1

FIRST SUNDAY OF ADVENT

(Year C; Jeremiah 33:14–16; 1 Thessalonians 3:12–4:2;
Luke 21:25–28, 34–36)

The appearance of the violet vestments this morning signals the beginning of a new liturgical year and of a new liturgical season, for today is the first Sunday of Advent. The violet replaces the green of Ordinary Time. The violet is a darker color and a somber one, signifying a time not of joy, but of preparation at once serious and grave, meditative and penitential, for joyful mysteries soon to be commemorated.

In one respect the Advent liturgies can be, on occasion, somewhat puzzling. For the seasonal Scripture readings appear to roll into one, three different comings of the Lord Christ, and they do not rigorously distinguish among them.

There is His first coming, as Savior in His Incarnation. It is to this that the Lord God is apparently referring through the lips of Jeremiah in the passage that is this day's Old Testament selection. "'Behold, the days are coming,' says the Lord, 'when I will fulfill the promise I made to the house of Israel and the house of Judah. In those days I will cause a righteous branch to spring forth from David.'"

Then there will be His second coming, as judge, at life's end first, and again as the great king on the last day when He will judge the living and the dead. It is apparently of this final coming that the Lord Christ speaks in that narrative from St. Luke's Gospel which we have just read. "There will be signs in the sun and the moon and the stars — the powers of the heavens will be shaken … and they will see the Son of Man coming in a cloud with great power and glory."

No reference is made in this day's Mass to His third coming, but there is on other occasions. This is that quiet, gratuitous, continuous coming among us in that supernatural indwelling for which grace is the necessary disposition. Our Savior Himself speaks of this coming in St. John's Gospel. "If anyone loves me, I will come to him, and my Father will come to him, and we will take up our abode with him" were His words to His chosen twelve at the Last Supper.[1]

No matter if the liturgy so intermingles its references to these comings. For the Church's primary concern is a practical one, the preparation on the part of Christ's followers, and for all three comings the preparation is essentially the same: a striving for Christian goodness that is earnest and persevering; a spirit of penance and reparation for evil done and for good left undone — the offenses that occasioned His coming in the first place.

To the point are Our Savior's concluding directives in the latter part of today's Gospel: "Take heed to yourselves lest your heart be weighed down with dissipation and drunkenness and the cares of this life ... watch at all times, praying that you may have strength." To the point also is St. Paul's injunction to his Christians of Thessalonica in today's second reading: "May the Lord make you increase and abound in love for one another and for all men ... that He may establish your hearts unblamable in holiness before Our God and Father, at the coming of Our Lord Jesus," and "As you learned from us how to live and to please God ... you do so more and more."

Yet the fact remains that it is Christmas that is approaching, and it is the first coming, the Incarnation, that we are looking forward to and that the Church would have us prepare ourselves for; it is to the wonder of this mystery that at Advent time the Church would have us direct our attention and the prayer of our heart.

St. Paul in the second chapter of his epistle to the Christians of Philippi speaks of the Incarnation and there refers to this mystery in terms suggestive of a humiliation, an abasement on the part of the Word Eternal. Urging his Christians to humility, he reminds them, "Let that mind be in you which is in Christ Jesus, who being in the form of God

---

[1] cf. Jn 14:23.

did not deem it theft to be equal to God, but He poured Himself out, taking the form of a servant, being made in the likeness of men, and in habit found as a man."[2]

The Apostle of course speaks the truth. That the Divine Son should become one of His creatures, and not one of the most excellent kind either, is the supreme act of humility. It is also, nonetheless, as St. Thomas points out, in a very real sense a most natural thing for God to do.

In the first article of the first question in the Tertia Pars of the *Summa Theologiae*, the theologian addresses himself to the question "Whether it was right, fitting — *utrum fuerit conveniens* — that God become man," and resolves the question so posed, simply and clearly in the very nature of God Himself.

It is fitting enough for man to reason, says St. Thomas, because this flows naturally from the very definition of his nature; to reason is something man is rightly expected to do. In similar vein, anything will be suitable to God and fitting to Him which in like manner can be said to flow from His essence. But the very essence of God as infinite perfection is goodness. Whatever therefore is proper to goodness as such will be the kind of thing that will belong naturally to God from His very essence. But our experience attests to it that if goodness as such has any proper characteristic, it is that it is *sui diffusivum*: it tends to burst from its confines, to spread out, to share and communicate itself. Our desires to share our joys, the tendency of life to communicate life, are cases in point; so too are good teachers, good musicians, and good cooks, all of whom spread goodness.

It is this tendency on the part of Divine goodness to share and communicate itself that accounts for creation in the first place.

But if it is consonant with the Divine nature, as good, so to communicate goodness by creation, it is even more consonant with that same Divine nature, as the greatest good, to communicate that Divine goodness in the greatest possible way. And there is a way possible for God to communicate goodness to man, greater even than by creation, and this is so to unite a human nature with Himself as to make with the infinite God one person. Such a communication as this is perfectly in harmony

---

[2]Phil 2:5–7.

with the Divine goodness — just the kind of thing, in other words, that God as infinite goodness might be expected to do.

The Collect prayer of this day's Mass suggests the aspirations of our hearts that are the fitting response to this overwhelming mystery and appropriate to this Advent time: "Father in heaven … increase our longing for Christ Our Savior and give us the strength to grow in love, that the dawn of His coming may find us rejoicing in His presence and welcoming the light of His truth."

2

SECOND SUNDAY OF ADVENT

(Year A; Matthew 3:1–12; Matthew 11:7–11)

On one occasion considerably later than the events recorded in today's Gospel selection, Our Divine Lord Himself was conversing with a group about John the Baptist and referring back to those days in the beginning when John began to preach in the Jordan wilderness. Recalling this time, He asked them, "What did you go out in the desert to see?"

They knew full well what they went out to see in those early days. They went out to see a man clothed simply. A leather girdle he wore, and camel's hair did not mean luxury then.

They knew not, most likely, that his conception had been announced, and that by Gabriel. They were ignorant that his name had been dictated by heaven and his birth attended by portents. But they must have realized, even then at least in some vague sort of way, that this was a man "great before the Lord … filled with the Holy Spirit, even from his mother's womb."[1] The man they went out to see was no reed shaken in the wind. He was a rugged man, a man with character written all over his face, a stranger to pretence, humbug, phoniness, pomp, hypocrisy, and cant. A simple — but this is miles from stupid — man, a direct man who thought straight thoughts and spoke them plainly and unmistakably.

What they saw there by the Jordan was an utterly dedicated man, dedicated to a cause he saw as greater than himself. His very dedication gives the lie to our own age whose malaise is a passion for self-fulfillment. This was the man they went out to see.

---

[1]Lk 1:15.

But they went out to hear in those days, rather than to see. He was a preacher by calling. This was his God-given work, and he was good at it. The crowds came, and they kept coming, and they kept coming back. High and low they came, Pharisees and Sadducees, ordinary sinners, priests and Levites, even one theological security delegation. They came from all over the region: Jerusalem, the Jordan country; from urbia, suburbia, exurbia.

The man who preached had no ideas of grandeur. He claimed to be no more than the instrument of one who was coming, the voice of one crying in the desert, not worthy to loosen His sandal. When the time came he did what it is so difficult for even a dedicated man to do: he stepped down, yielding his fame and function and fruit to another. "Greater than I … He must increase, and I must decrease."[2]

There was nothing hesitant and nothing timorous about the delivery of his message though it was by no means a popular message. "Do penance; bring forth fruits worthy of penance." Change your heart. Measure up. "For even now the axe is laid to the root of the trees. Every tree that fails to bring forth good fruit will be cut down."

This simplicity of his, his directness, honesty, courage, his utter dedication: What did it get him? It got him the admiration of the crowds. But this he knew wouldn't last. This he could take for what it was — not much. This he could handle and get on with the job. It got him the fear and respect of Herod Antipas, who locked him up indefinitely but liked to hear him. It got him the venomous hatred of such appalling people as Herod's wife, who would gladly murder him if she got the chance, and she did. It got him a sickening, hideous, and inglorious death at the behest of a cheap dancing girl.

It also got him unstinted praise and approval from the only one whose praise and approval mean anything, then or now: Jesus Christ, Our Lord. "What went you out into the desert to see? A reed shaken in the wind?" No, not that. "A man clothed in soft garments?" Not that either. "A prophet? Yes, and more than a prophet. This is he of whom it is written: 'Behold I send my messenger before thy face, who shall make ready thy way before thee.' Amen, I say to you, among those born of

---

[2] cf. Mt 3:11; Jn 3:30.

woman, there has not arisen a greater than John the Baptist."

It got him the undying memory of Christ's Church, who in these days of preparation for the coming of Christ bids us turn our respectful and reverent gaze once again to this giant among the saints, the last of the prophets, and the link between the two Testaments, whose task it was to prepare the world for the first coming of the Savior.

3

IMMACULATE CONCEPTION

(Luke 1:26–38)

Among St. Thomas' briefer theological works is his explanation of our most familiar prayer, the Hail Mary.[1] At the beginning of this exposition he remarks that in Old Testament times it was a great thing — *erat valde magnum* — that an angel should appear to man. Abraham is a classic case in point. As we read in the eighteenth chapter of Genesis, three angels paid him a visit in the valley of Mambre, "as he was sitting by the door of his tent, in the very heat of the day … As soon as he saw them he ran to meet them and adored down to the ground … 'I will fetch a little water,' he said, 'and wash your feet.'"[2]

Abraham's manners on the occasion were impeccable. For, as St. Thomas remarks, it is a matter for highest praise that man should thus show reverence, respect, and deference to one so high above him on all counts as the angel is.

But contrarily, that the angel should be the one to manifest respect, reverence, and deference to the human, this was something unheard of in Old Testament times until Gabriel, being come in to Mary, reverently saluted her: "*Ave.*"

Rightly so, for this time — the only time — the excellence, the superiority, was, and is, on the side of the human, the Queen of Angels.

"*Ave gratia plena.*" The reason for the "*ave*" is in the two words that follow it. It is as if the angel had said, as St. Thomas expressed it, "For this do I defer, for in grace you are my superior."

---

[1]*Opuscula Theologica, In Salutationem Angelicam Expositio*; cf. *The Three Greatest Prayers* (Manchester, NH: Sophia Institute Press, 1990).　　[2]Gen 18: 1–2, 4.

"He who is mighty has done great things for me" were Mary's words to her cousin Elizabeth.[3] This He did for the Mother of the Incarnate Word: He preserved her free from original sin, first of all. In her were none of those disastrous effects of Adam's fall that so stain and warp the rest of us, turning us upside down, so to speak, so that in us the baser tends to rule the nobler. We are all painfully aware of these calamitous consequences. We fall so often; we fall short even of our own aspirations, modest as they are; we disappoint ourselves, our fellow man, and God.

In the Blessed Mother there were none of these woeful scars. On the contrary, from the beginning of her existence she was "*gratia plena*." Grace means union with God; grace means the indwelling of Father, Son, and Holy Spirit. Grace means wisdom to see clearly the good and sort it out from the evil; grace means strength unfailingly to do the former and avoid the latter.

Fullness of grace means utter sinlessness. "We know," says St. Augustine, "that grace in abundance to conquer sin on all fronts was lavished on her who merited to conceive and bear Him whom all know had no sin." She never disappointed, and she alone among all of us never had occasion to say on her own account a Confiteor or an Act of Contrition. "Thou art all fair, my beloved" is the prophecy in the Canticle, "and there is no stain in thee."[4]

Fullness of grace means virtue most attractive and appealing, perfection of manners; in her case, feminine manners. Through the singular grace that was hers, Mary was the mother most amiable, mother most admirable, and in her God's idea of what a human being can be did not perish. In the entire history of our race, she stands out as the one perfect lady.

Who so excels in grace excels in divine life, and so excels simply. Rightly then did the angel defer.

We read in the Acts of Pope Pius IX:

On December 8, 1854, surrounded by a large gathering of cardinals and bishops, with the whole world applauding, we solemnly pronounce and decree that the doctrine which holds that the most

---

[3]Lk 1:49.   [4]Cant 4:7.

Blessed Virgin Mary, in the first instant of her conception, by a singular grace and privilege granted by Almighty God, was preserved free from every stain of original sin, is a doctrine revealed by God, and therefore to be firmly, and constantly believed by all the faithful.[5]

Today we commemorate and celebrate that singular privilege of the Blessed Mother's. That that commemoration be the more solemn and serious, the Church obliges the faithful to hear Mass on this day.

"*Ave*," Gabriel greeted her. In the angel's spirit we pay our reverence to her today and join with the angels and saints in rejoicing that one human being has been so favored by God and has risen to such loveable and attractive heights of human perfection.

We rejoice for ourselves too, secure in the confidence that this most holy Mother of Christ extends her mother's love and the power of a mother's intercession to all the members of her Son's Mystical Body, and that means every one of us.

[5]cf. Apostolic Constitution on the Dogma of the Immaculate Conception, *Ineffabilis Deus*, 62.

4

THIRD SUNDAY OF ADVENT

(Year C; Zephaniah 3:14–18; Philippians 4:4–7; Luke 3:10–18)

Back in the days of the *ecclesia antiqua* — maybe four or five years ago — there were two Sundays in the liturgical year when the Church prescribed for Mass rose-colored vestments, should a given parish be so fortunate as to own a set. Of these Sundays, one occurred in the latter part of Lent: "Laetare Sunday," we called it, and perhaps still do. The other was this present day, the third Sunday of Advent. This also enjoyed its own proper title, for we called it "Gaudete Sunday." Both were named for the opening word of the Mass: "*Laetare Jerusalem*" in one case, "*Gaudete in Domino*" in the other. "*Laetare*," "*gaudete*" — the words are fairly synonymous. Both mean rejoice. The rose color represented a sort of compromise between the somber violet, symbolic of Advent's penitential spirit, and the brighter hues suggested by the theme of the particular Mass and the texts thereof.

In today's Mass the Gospel continues last week's narrative. It returns us to the banks of the Jordan in the Judean wilderness. John the Baptist is again the focus of attention. The crowds sought his counsel on moral matters. Through his replies the Church reminds us of Advent's proper project — by perfecting ourselves, to prepare for the coming of the Lord.

The Old Testament reading, however, and the epistle have a theme of their own. It is this theme that the opening antiphon introduces: "Rejoice in the Lord."

"Shout for joy, O daughter of Zion," proclaims the prophet Zephaniah in the first reading, "sing joyfully, O Israel." And in the second Paul instructs the Christians of Philippi, "Rejoice in the Lord always. I say it again, rejoice."

Undeniably there are moments of transfiguring happiness in every life. A crushing burden is lifted from our shoulders, a striking success rewards our efforts, we experience kindness and are warmed by love. These are peak periods of human existence. They are the result of some considerable and desired goods, attained at last and present, of whose presence we are keenly aware. But the fact is that these moments of happiness are as transient as their causes, and we wonder if this is the type of thing Paul had in mind when he wrote the people of Philippi, "I want you to be happy, always happy in the Lord."

Whether this twentieth century world of ours is actually more confused and depraved than the past is not all that clear. But at any rate the confusion and depravity are such as to make the notion of Christian joy a challenging one in this, our day. In such a messed up world, what can anyone with eyes and half a brain find to be joyous about?

If the Apostle urged his Christians of Philippi to this blessed condition of spirit we call joy, and if today the Church repeats that message, it must be because there are at hand, then and now, reasons that rest fast in faith, reasons so compelling as to leave no place for the contrary; glumness is out. For all that is good, including the deep content the Apostle is talking about, we need God's assisting grace. Helped thereby, we need to deepen and preserve, preserve and deepen, our awareness of these reasons. Fundamentally, the reason for our Christian joy is something special, in fact unique. The reason for our Christian joy is Christ.

As Catholics we have reason for lasting and deep joy. We have only to grasp and appreciate the Incarnation and all the wealth of comfort that this overwhelming truth has. The Incarnation persuades us once and for all of the boundless love of God. "God so loved the world," writes St. John, "that He gave His only-begotten."[1] The Incarnation means that God Himself is now one of us; God is now our brother in the flesh, has a mother. The Second Person of the Triune God emptied Himself to

[1] Jn 3:16.

assume the condition of a slave, to become as men are. It is not as if we had a high priest who is incapable of feeling our weakness with us, but we have one who has been surrounded by temptation even as we are, though He is without sin.[2] The Incarnation has given new value and fresh beauty to all life.

There is reason for joy, too, in the realization of the love that was Christ's. Jesus of Nazareth showed toward people the warmest, most patient, most disinterested love: there come to mind the Apostles, Peter in particular, who denied Him thrice; Magdalene; and the tax collector Zacchaeus. Even for those who hated Him, He had forgiveness. There is joy in the conviction that we, such as we are, are presently loved by Christ. Sincerely we respond to that love.

There is reason for joy, too, in the promises of Christ. We need but to take them seriously and ponder them: "He who believes and is baptized shall be saved." "Ask and it shall be given to you; search and you will find; knock and the door will be opened to you." "If anyone declares himself for me in the presence of man, the Son of Man will declare Himself for him in the presence of God's angels." "Come to me, all you who labor and are overburdened, and I shall give you rest."[3]

For some such reasons as these, St. Paul says to the Philippians that he wants them happy. Reasons such as these he would have them take to heart. Each year on this third Sunday of Advent the Church recalls and repeats this, his message. The reasons still obtain, and the simple fact of the matter is that on the face of this green earth there never has been any surer sign of the presence of God than deep and lasting joy.

[2] cf. Phil 2:7; Heb 4:15   [3] Mk 16:16; Mt 7:7; Lk 12:8; Mt 11:28.

5

FOURTH SUNDAY OF ADVENT

(Year C; Luke 1:39–45)

If Scripture had left us uninformed on this subject, it might make interesting speculation to wonder just what was the first thing the Mother of Christ did after Gabriel's momentous announcement to her and her own equally momentous *fiat*: "Be it done unto me according to thy word." But we do know. She made the four-day journey from Nazareth in the north to Judea in the south to spend time — three months as it turned out — with her well-placed kinswoman Elizabeth.

The event commemorated in this day's Gospel narrative is now the second joyful mystery of our Rosary. Why this visitation? The inspired word supplies us with the answer, although Elizabeth herself asked the question: "Whence is this to me that the mother of my God should come to me?"

A momentous event had just come to pass in Mary's life, and not just in her life but in the history of the world. The Mother of Christ might just have felt the need to speak to someone — not her gossiping neighbors, whom later events proved to be a sorry lot anyway; not Joseph, for clearly Mary sensed that that sticky part of the problem had to be left to God. And Gabriel had in fact actually dropped a hint about Elizabeth: "Behold, your cousin Elizabeth has conceived, and it is now the sixth month of her that is called barren."

There was more to it of course. Our Lady's three-month stay more or less terminated with the birth of Elizabeth's child. Surely Mary intended to be of service to her kinswoman: like Son, like mother. Above all, one is drawn to suspect that the Mother of Christ powerfully experienced an impulse which friends and servants of Christ — St. Paul, for one — have experienced ever since: the intense desire to share Christ with others. In any case Mary became the first Christopher, Christ-bearer, the first apostle, the first joyful herald to announce the good news of Christ.

About Elizabeth, St. Luke makes a statement that must be noted: "She was filled with the Holy Spirit." The Evangelist will never let Christ's followers lose sight of the fact that the Holy Spirit is at work in the earliest events of Christ's life; on this he insists again and again. Of John the Baptist, he says, "He was filled with the Holy Spirit even from his mother's womb," and of Mary herself, "The Holy Spirit will come upon you," and of Zachary, "Zachary was filled with the Holy Spirit," and later of Simeon, "The Holy Spirit rested on him. It had been revealed to him by the Holy Spirit."[1]

He works through whom He wills, and through whom He wills He accomplishes His great purposes. We find the mystery of His ways re-echoed by Mary in her *Magnificat*: "He hath exalted the lowly … and the rich He hath sent away empty."[2]

"Blessed are you among women" was Elizabeth's greeting, words uttered then for the first time, and "Blessed is she who believed that there would be a fulfillment of what was spoken to her from the Lord."

It is fitting that on this last Sunday before Christmas the Church should, by this Gospel narrative, bid us turn the direction of our thoughts and affections on our mother who is so blessed among women.

In particular, during this passing period when confusion and humbug appear to prevail in schools theological, Christmas is the time to remind ourselves that the Blessed Mother of Christ has not been quietly edged to the wings of the Christian spectacular because of faint disapproval in scattered members of the audience. If anyone suspects that Mary of Nazareth has had her day in Christian history, let him steadily regard the Nativity scene as recorded by St. Luke. Our Lady, radiant and gentle as ever, remains the key figure, for she is the mother of God Incarnate in the manger. She is here to stay.

---

[1]Lk 1:15; Lk 1:35; Lk 1:67; Lk 2:25.   [2]Lk 1:52–53.

CHRISTMAS

6

CHRISTMAS

MIDNIGHT MASS

(Isaiah 9:1–6; Luke 2:1–14)

This Mass we are presently offering is the Church's Christmas Mass at midnight. In the Collect prayer that we offered just a few moments ago, we began by addressing ourselves to God, our Creator and Lord, in these words: "Father, you make this holy night radiant with the splendor of Jesus Christ our light. We welcome Him as Lord, the true light of the world."

If we should then turn our attention to the Collect prayer of this day's second Mass, the Mass at dawn, we find that this opens in much the same vein: "Father, we are filled with the new light by the coming of your Word among us."

In fact this appealing image of light we find everywhere in the Nativity liturgy. We heard a few moments ago, for instance, the Old Testament selection of this Mass, taken from Isaiah. The prophet envisages the Messiah's coming as the dawn of a great light in a world that without the Redeemer is simply in irremediable darkness. "The people who walked in darkness," he proclaimed, "have seen a great light; upon those who dwelt in the land of gloom a light has shone."

The Gospel narrative we read just a few moments ago from St. Luke recounts the details so familiar and cherished — the City of David, the carpenter from Nazareth and his youthful wife, the improvised crib, and then the baby boy who is God Incarnate. And again the reference to light: "There were shepherds watching their flocks in the fields … when the glory of God shone round about them."

In the stable itself there may have been precious little light in the physical sense, but in another sense there was no darkness either. The Light that shone in the poor manger was light enough to illumine the whole world. For "this is the true light that illumines every man coming into this world,"[1] St. John will one day write of Jesus of Nazareth, and He would in time, at a feast of tabernacles in Jerusalem, Himself proclaim: "I am the light of the world."[2]

It is truth that is the light of the mind. Enlightened by truth, man can see his way and is secure and unafraid. He can direct his steps with sureness and a security born of certainty, and direct them to happiness in the next world and in this. Such truth Incarnate Wisdom came to teach and would indeed teach — on the Mount and from the boat, and in the synagogues and in the temple of God. "I am the truth," He would proclaim,[3] and hence also the light.

But the truth He taught does us no good if we accept it not, and so He offered Himself as the victim on Calvary, winning for us with grace the gift of faith. Through that gift of faith we make His truth our own and walk in His light.

Christ has come and the world need no longer be in darkness; the truth is at hand.

For this gift — that He has given the light and called us thereto — we must needs thank Him at Christmas time. Ours it is as well to pray most earnestly for the world that ignores the light that is Christ, or rejects Him, and so can do naught in the darkness but stumble in fear or rashly plunge to its own destruction.

In this same Collect prayer of the midnight Mass we make just one petition: "Bring us to eternal joy in the kingdom of heaven."

We are all keenly aware of the transience of Christmas. So much time is spent in anticipation of our celebration of the Nativity, and so much time and energy, both, in our preparation thereof, that it comes as something of a surprise that the day is no longer than any other. Christmas is a peaceful, gentle, and happy time. The harshness departs from life; the raucous, strident noises are stilled, animosities allayed. Once again it is "silent night, holy night," and there is "peace on earth,"

[1]Jn 1:9.   [2]Jn 8:12.   [3]Jn 14:6.

for so hallowed and so gracious is the time. And then it is over, and the clank and the clamor resume, and the burdens are taken up as before.

And so the prayer of the Church is as it is. Christmas passes; we set not our hearts on the passing day but pray for what is permanent. We must walk in the light that is Christ. Our prayer is that we may arrive at eternal joy in the kingdom of heaven, that we may be ever merry in the light that does not fail or fade.

7

HOLY FAMILY

(Ecclesiasticus 3:3–7, 14–17)

My dear friends, this Sunday, the Sunday after Christmas day, in the calendar of the Church is the feast of the Holy Family. This is a day when we look upon Jesus, Mary, and Joseph not so much as individuals whom we might emulate and to whom we pray, but as a family. Humbly we regard them as just that, a family, and we address to them our prayers.

It makes sense that this feast should be observed so close to Christmas day. With the first Christmas the Holy Family began; at this time of year the infancy of Christ is still fresh in our minds. By a kind of happy coincidence this day falls, too, at a time of year when family means most to us. For Christmas is a family time. It is a time when we want to be with our families; for the most part we hate the thought of being apart from them. Some of us travel six thousand miles round trip to be with our family. At this time of year too, more than at others, our heart goes out to those who have no family to be with.

The women's libbers, evidently, would do away with all this. For they would free women from the restraints of the home, and without woman in the home there can be no family. We wonder: What do they have to offer to take its place?

In the entrance prayer of today's Mass, we first address ourselves to the Lord Christ. We recall: "You sanctified home life with untold virtues by being subject to Mary and Joseph." Then we beg from Him the help of His parents: "May they assist us to imitate the example of your Holy Family so that we may share with them their eternal happiness."

Thus in this prayer we profess that we see a connection between imitating the example of Joseph, Mary, and Jesus and our eternal happiness. Such a connection is clear enough. For hominess such as theirs, studied, loved, followed out, can lead only to the eternal happiness of heaven.

We need to realize, too, that this eternal happiness for which we pray ought to have its actual and very real beginnings in this life itself. Within the good home, within the good family, God's human creatures can attain and enjoy — and there are those who do, ordinarily and generally speaking — the contentment of the good home, which is the deepest allotted to man in this vale of tears.

It seems most reasonable and logical, on the face of it, that this is one subject on which the priest is least qualified to speak. After all, he never has been faced with the myriad trials and tribulations and complexities involved in running a home.

There is of course much truth in this. But to some extent we do get around. There are visits in the line of duty; there is hospitality shared. Most of us are privileged, from time to time, to witness and to share in homes where a deep contentment and the sheer joy of being together fill every nook and cranny. This is what it can be.

We find it to be the case that where such solid happiness prevails, the first part of today's prayer is fulfilled too: "You sanctified home life with untold virtues by being subject to Mary and Joseph." The happiness of the home is not something that simply falls into our laps, a gift from Dame Fortune, as it were. It is not even a totally gratuitous gift from God. Family life has this much in common with rectory life and religious community life: it is what the people in it make it to be.

"The Lord sets a father in honor over his children," we read in today's first lesson; "a mother's authority He confirms over her sons." Wise and firm, enlightened and persevering guidance on the part of the parents is far from easy, but it pays dividends in time. In the prayer of today's Mass we pray that we imitate the virtues of the Holy Family. We have the commandments of God and the Church that spell out this imitation more in detail. Consideration of one for all and each for each, interest in each other, these are among the untold virtues with which the Lord sanctified home life and without which the happy home simply cannot be. It all comes about easily enough where there is deep love, for this makes sacrifice bearable and even easy; this makes happiness possible even in injury and sickness and in the face of "the slings and arrows of outrageous fortune."

The women's libbers whether they realize it or not would destroy the family. Let them propose then some more human, more natural way to raise human beings. Nothing else has ever been found to work. Let them remember that in freeing human creatures from the constraints of family life, they are also freeing us from the rewards thereof — the happiness of life in the good family.

8

HOLY FAMILY (2)

(Year B; Luke 2:22–40)

The Gospel selection we have just read is St. Luke's account, the original and the source of what since the days of St. Dominic has become the fourth joyful mystery of the Rosary, the Presentation in the Temple. The narrative focuses on the Holy Family, whose feast we celebrate this day: "When the day came to purify them according to the Law of Moses," writes the Evangelist, "Mary and Joseph brought Jesus up to Jerusalem that He might be presented to the Lord."

"When the day came to purify them," writes St. Luke. The law apparently called for purification of both — Jesus and Mary.

This is a mystery of the infancy that St. Thomas directs his attention to in the third and fourth articles of Question 37 in the Tertia Pars, a question which is about the circumcision of Christ and other *legalia* — prescriptions of the law — observed in His regard.

In the third article the theologian asks "*Utrum convenienter fuerit Christus in templo oblatus*" — "Whether it was suitable, right, fitting that Christ have been offered in the temple."

On the face of it, the question so posed would seem to call for a negative answer.

In the first place, as we read the law in the thirteenth chapter of Exodus, it appears to have no application in Our Savior's regard: "Sanctify unto me every first-born male that openeth the womb among the children of Israel, as well of men as of beasts, for they are all mine."[1] But the Mother of Christ remained virginal before, during, and after His birth:

[1]Ex 13:2

so miraculous was its manner that in a very real sense He may be said not to have opened her womb.

"They brought Him to Jerusalem," writes St. Luke, "to present Him to the Lord." But nothing could seem more superfluous than to present to God one already so present as to be united in the unity of a single person. How does one present to God the man who is God?

Christ Himself, moreover, came on earth as the victim *par excellence*, the *hostia principalis*, says St. Thomas, whom all other sacrifices prefigured, and whose own sacrifice would redeem and sanctify all else. What could appear sillier than to offer a pair of doves for His redemption and consecration?

The law of Moses involved in the presentation was, as St. Thomas explains it, a twofold law. There was first the general precept involved. Every mother, whether her child be son or daughter, first or subsequent, was obliged when the prescribed days of purgation were finished, to pay a visit to the temple. There the law called for one offering in expiation of sin and then for another by way of a certain consecration of the child to God (a consecration to participation in holy things, perhaps prefiguring our own baptismal character, that indelible sign that consecrates us for participation in divine worship). Of this law we read in the book of Leviticus.

The second precept was the more special one. It concerned only first-born males, whether sons or whether first-born of the flocks and herds. These God considered as belonging in a special way to Himself. To free His chosen people from Egypt's bondage He had slain the eldest son of the Egyptian families and the first-born of all their domestic beasts. Consequently the first-born was to be offered to God. Such was the law.

Jesus of Nazareth was and is Incarnate God, the lawgiver Himself, the almighty and infinite recipient of all sacrifices and oblations. He was born in a manner most miraculous, foreign to any trace of passion that might call for expiation or redemption. Clearly He was not bound by the law.

But St. Paul instructed the Christians of Galatia, and through them, us, that just as Christ was born in the fullness of time, at that time namely that He Himself willed, so He willed to be born of a woman; so also He willed to be born under the law. This was His own will, His own choice. And this for a reason: "that He might redeem those who were under the law."[2] Not for His good did He will so to be born, that He might be bettered by life in accord with the law, as was the aim in regard to the other sons of Israel, but for the good of the people, for the good of the world, for our good.

Given this will on His part to be born under the law, a will ordered to our good, then what He did was suitable, fitting, right. He was born of a woman: hence the sin offering and the holocaust as the law pre-scribed. He was a first-born: hence the turtle doves according to the law of the first-born.

He was born under the law to redeem those who were under the law. St. Athanasius offers as an instance: "For our sake was He offered to God, that we might learn from Him to present ourselves to God."

Whatever sacrifices were prescribed by the Old Law were fig-ures of Him, the *vera hostia*, true victim. There in the temple, then, as St. Thomas remarks, the figure was united to the truth, and through the truth the figure was approved. Truth Incarnate, there, while still an infant, gave His own wordless stamp of approbation to the figures of the Old Law.

His mother, too, obeyed the law, although in her it found no rea-son for application.

The Lord Christ is God Incarnate, and in Him has always dwelt the fullness of grace. The act of obedience to the demands of the law was for Him a voluntary and loving act of humility. Accordingly St. Thomas reasons, "Just as the plenitude of grace flowed from Christ to His mother, so it was fitting that the mother be conformed to the humility of the Son." For, "It is to the humble that God gives grace," as we read in the letter of James.[3] And therefore just as Christ, although He was not subject to the law, willed to undergo circumcision and the other burdens of the law to give an example of humility and obedience and to approve the law, for the same reason He willed that His mother

---

[2]Gal 4:5.   [3]James 4:6.

fulfill the rituals of the law, to which, however, she was not subject. The principle here is a simple one: like Son, like mother.

9

JANUARY 1

MARY, MOTHER OF GOD

(Proverbs 13:22)

In the revised liturgical calendar this first day of January, the octave of Christmas, formerly the commemoration of the circumcision, is now dedicated to our Blessed Lady. January 1 remains as it was — a holy day of obligation — but now it enjoys as its formal title "The Solemnity of Mary, Mother of God." It is fitting that during this Nativity season and on the first day of the New Year the Church should bid us direct our thoughts and affections toward her who can never be too much in the forefront of our thoughts and affections, Mary, the Mother of Christ and our mother.

"Blessed art thou among women" is the tribute we pay her in our most familiar prayer to her, and we add "Blessed is the fruit of thy womb."

"The substance of the sinner shall be preserved for the just one," we read in the Book of Proverbs; a truth, this, that we find realized when we compare Eve, the common mother of us all, with Mary of Nazareth, our mother as Christians. Eve's substance was what she set her heart on, in that fruit to which, at the serpent's bidding, she turned her attentions and the affections of her heart. What she wanted in that fruit were goods she wanted for herself; she was disappointed in all; she attained none. "Be it done to me according to thy word," said Mary.[1] She sought nothing for herself but found in the fruit of her womb all the blessings that escaped Eve.

Eve took the fruit and ate of it at the tempter's urging. She expected first of all what he promised her: "You shall be like gods, knowing good

---

[1] Lk 1:38.

and evil."[2] He lied, of course; he always lies because he is a liar and the father of lies. Eve was disappointed. She became not like God but immeasurably less like Him. She sinned and in sinning parted from God her Savior and was driven from paradise.

But what Eve attained not, the Blessed Mother did find in the fruit of her womb. Not only she, but all her Son's faithful followers. For through Christ we are united with God and through His grace transformed into the likeness of the Divinity. "When He will appear, we shall be like Him," writes St. John in his first epistle, "because we shall see Him as He is."[3]

In the fruit she took and ate, Eve looked for delight. She encountered instead her introduction to misery. But in the fruit of the Virgin Mary we do find our true contentment and our salvation, which is eternal delight: "My yoke is sweet"; "Who eats of My flesh has eternal life."[4]

Eve's fruit was pleasing to the eye, as we read in Genesis: "Fair to the eyes and delightful to behold."[5] But Mary's fruit is immeasurably more beautiful, for on Him the angels delight to gaze: "Beautiful beyond the sons of men," proclaims the Psalmist,[6] and the author of Hebrews gives the reason: "because He is the splendor of the Father's glory."[7]

What Eve then could not find in the fruit that she made hers, no sinner ever finds in his sin. And therefore the goods that the wise man seeks, he seeks in the blessed fruit that Mary bore.

Blessed indeed is He, for He is "full of grace and truth," and "of His fullness we have all received, grace for grace."[8] Most abundantly of all did she receive who is closest to Him of all — His mother. And accordingly since the fruit of her womb is so blessed, she herself is blessed among women.

---

[2]Gen 3:5.   [3]1 Jn 3:2.   [4]Mt 11:30; Jn 6:54. [5]Gen 3:6.   [6]Ps 45:2.   [7]Heb 1:3.
[8]Jn 1:14, 16.

10

FEAST OF THE HOLY NAME

There are many ways in which loving eyes may look upon the Lord Christ. He may be seen as God, and He may be known as man, for He is both. We may regard Him as teacher, or good shepherd, or king, or priest, or redeemer, or mystical food, or everlasting conqueror. He is all of this, is Our Lord and Master Jesus Christ, and infinitely more.

The liturgy of the Christmas season looks upon Christ, Our Lord, in a special way: as the Light. "God, who made this holy night to blaze with brilliance of the true Light, grant, we beg, that as we celebrate the mysteries of this Light on earth, so may we share His joys in heaven." "Grant, we beg of you, Almighty God, that as we are filled with the new light of your Incarnate Word, so there may shine in our deeds what by faith flames in our hearts."

St. Bernard in a sermon on the Canticle of Canticles[1] considers the words of the bride to the husband: "Your name is oil poured out."[2] St. Bernard applies these words to the name of Jesus. He finds that the name of Jesus is oil poured out in three ways. One of them is this: oil, insofar as it is fuel for a lamp, is a source of light, and it is in the light of the name of Jesus that God has called us to His own admirable light.

It was this holy name, St. Bernard says, that the Apostle Paul was commanded to bear as a light before kings and the Gentiles and the sons of Israel, and he bore this name as a light. With this name he illumined his native land, and he cried out everywhere, "You were once in darkness, now you are a light in the Lord. Night has passed, the day has

---

[1]*St. Bernard's Sermons on the Canticle of Canticles*, Sermon XV, "On the Name of Jesus."
[2]Cant 1:3

approached. Let us therefore put off the works of darkness and put on
the armor of light."[3] And he showed to all this light, preaching everywhere Jesus, and Him crucified. St. Bernard remarks how the light of this
name must have shone forth and dazzled the eyes of the bystanders when
St. Peter said to the cripple, "Silver and gold I have none, but in the
name of the Lord Jesus Christ, arise and walk,"[4] and what had been two
useless encumbering appendages became on the spot solid legs of bone
and muscle and sinew.

Our Lord Himself said it: "I am the light of the world."[5] There may
have been precious little light in the stable-cave at Bethlehem, but there
was no darkness either. The Light that shone in the poor manger was
light enough to illumine the whole world.

This is now the third Christmas time of the new era of sacred
history opened by Vatican Council II. Following the monumental
Constitution on the Church, we Catholics are able to glimpse — as never
before — what it means to be born in Christ.

The Constitution's basic motif is announced in its opening sentence: "Christ is the Light of Nations." All of us, the Council reminds
us, share a common dignity from our rebirth in Christ, with the same
grace of children of God, with the same call to holiness. This call carries
with it no slight responsibility. For it is precisely through us that Christ,
who is the light of the world, will progressively enlighten the whole of
human society.

If most of the world, not only in remote areas, still struggles in agonizing darkness, unable to see the light that we know has already been
given mankind, where lies the fault? Why doesn't that light reach every
man that comes into the world?

Why God left such an amount of His work to us is a mystery. The
Council invites us to change the world, to see that its goods are "more
equitably distributed," "to raise all of society to a better way of existence,"
"to wipe out every kind of separateness," "to be symbols of the living
God."[6] This is the Christmas blessing we need to pray for in our time: to
be channels, not blocks, of the light that is Christ.

---

[3]Eph 5:8; Rom 13:12.   [4]Acts 3:6.   [5]Jn 8:12.   [6]cf. Dogmatic Constitution on the
Church, *Lumen Gentium*, 36; 41; 28; 38.

11

EPIPHANY

(Ephesians 3:2–3, 5–6; Matthew 2:1–12)

The Gospel narrative on this feast of the Epiphany is St. Matthew's familiar account of the journey of the Magi, of their detour to Herod's lair and the delay that entailed, of their arrival finally at their goal: their adoration of the infant in the manger. Seen so, in isolation as it were, taken by itself, the episode appears as an engaging incident in the infancy of the Incarnate Word, but rather inconsequential overall, so far as our salvation is concerned. In fact the Magi, in a certain way, recall Melchizedek: they are mysterious figures; they enter the scriptural narrative; they disappear without a trace.

But the tradition of the Church has always regarded the Magi's call, their trek, and their adoration as a matter of supreme import; the Epiphany ranks with Christmas and Easter among the major celebrations of the liturgical year.

The true significance of Melchizedek appears in the Epistle to the Hebrews. He was a figure of the priesthood of Christ. Like him the Magi were also a figure. They were both a beginning and a kind of prophecy, and in this lies their special significance. What is of consequence is not so much that they were learned men, nor astrologers, nor wealthy, nor royalty themselves (if they were), nor that they were from afar, but that they were Gentiles.

Christ was born; the prophecies were fulfilled; the Messiah had at length come. It was imperative that this event of all events, the purpose and crown of all that had preceded, not remain hidden, but that it be manifested to men.

St. Thomas Aquinas, in the Tertia Pars, devotes an entire question — eight articles — to the subject of the manifestation of Christ's nativity.[1] In the sixth article he contemplates the order in which the birth of the Savior was actually made manifest. It was to shepherds that Our Lord's nativity was first announced, and that by angels; secondly His coming was made known to the Magi, by a star probably created and moved solely for that purpose; thirdly to Simeon and Anna, by a direct inspiration of the Holy Spirit thanks to which when the infant was presented in the temple they recognized Him for who He was.

Good theologian that he is, convinced that God has a reason not only for what He does but also for the order of steps in which He does it, St. Thomas investigates the reason for this particular sequence. He finds the explanation in a certain prefiguring on the part of Divine Providence. The shepherds, the Magi, Simeon and Anna — this sequence itself is a sort of prophecy. Through it God meant to disclose the order in which, in time, the faith of Christ would reach the world of men, an order the Jews of the time would never have surmised and whose very notion would have been a scandal had it been suggested.

For the faith of Christ would come to the Apostles first, and a few other Jews among whom there were but few powerful or noble or learned in the law; these the shepherds prefigured. Secondly the Gospel reached the Gentiles, consequent upon the labors of Paul and the Apostles. In His providence God ordained the Magi as the first of these and a figure of the rest. Only lastly, and we know not when, will the Gospel reach the bulk of the Jews, prefigured in those early days by Simeon and Anna.

Then in his eighth article St. Thomas wonders about the prudence of this westward trek of the Wise Men and of their adoration of the Infant Christ. "We have come to adore Him," they proclaimed — not to see, nor to visit, but to adore Him.

After all, the Magi were not Jews. There was no need for them to plod over hills and miles of desert to pay homage to a king newly born to that people. Besides, if one is so to honor a king, one waits until he

---

[1] IIIa, q. 36.

is regally installed; no one in his right mind bows to an infant in a stable. One step in their procedure appears as the height of foolishness: they announced the birth of a new king within the domain of an already actually reigning monarch, Herod — "that fox"[2] — heartless among the most heartless of tyrants, to whom a few more murders would be, as it were, as nothing.

Again St. Thomas finds the ultimate reason and true explanation of this entire episode in the Magi's role as figures, as foreshadowings of wonders later to come.

In some way not revealed in the Gospel, the Lord God communicated to them that the star would lead them to one King of the Jews, yet more than that. Like Abraham, they believed. They set out on their journey and persevered thereon. God in His providence withdrew the guidance of the star somewhere about Jerusalem. They did not abandon their quest; with diligence they found other means of direction; they persevered.

In all this, St. Thomas notes, quoting St. Augustine, the Magi were the *primitiae gentium*, the first fruits of the nations. In them dwelt and in them was manifest *in quodam praesagio*, as a kind of figure or prophetic token, all the faith and devotion of the peoples who would in the course of time believe in Christ and come to Him from the remotest corners of the earth. In the eyes of the world, this too is foolishness. But people of all nations have come with wisdom to the source of salvation, inspired, guided, directed by the Holy Spirit. The Magi were simply the first of them so to show reverence to Christ.

In the Magi was manifest also, notes the theologian, not only the welcoming of the nations into the kingdom, but more than that, even that heroic constancy that would in time characterize so many of the Gentiles who would profess Christ even unto death. Under Herod's very nose they openly avowed their purpose. Says Chrysostom, "When they pondered the future king, they did not fear the present king; as yet they had not seen Christ, and already they were prepared to die for Him."

In the passage which is the second reading of this Epiphany Mass,

---

[2] Lk 13:32.

St. Paul apprises his Christians of Ephesus of a mystery concealed from men in prior generations, now revealed to him and to God's holy apostles and prophets. Through the grace of God, these have come to see that the Gentiles are co-heirs, and of the same body, and co-partners in God's promise through the Gospel.

To this end the Apostle dedicated himself, becoming a slave of Christ, as he puts it, "for you Gentiles."[3] In this openness the New Dispensation differs radically from the Old, which was exclusive, limited to one people. It is this mark of Christ's kingdom that we call its catholicity. It is this same mark that the Magi prefigured, that Paul proclaimed, and which in the Church today is the reason for the joy of this Epiphany time.

[3]Eph 3:1.

12

BAPTISM OF CHRIST

(FIRST SUNDAY OF THE YEAR)

(Year A; Matthew 3:13–17)

It is only in recent years that there has been in the liturgical cycle a Sunday consecrated, explicitly and by name, to commemorate Our Savior's baptism. The event itself, at the beginning of Christ's public life, is familiar enough, and we have just read St. Matthew's account. Our Divine Lord came down from Galilee to the Jordan to be baptized by His cousin and precursor. As St. Thomas notes, the situation was similar to the sun rising, as it sometimes does, while the evening star is still in the sky.[1]

Clearly John's baptism was no sacrament; it was a baptism of penance. Just as clearly the Lord Christ, like us in all things save sin, had no need of it. Yet it was for reasons sound and sufficient that He came south from Galilee and bowed His head there in the Jordan.

There was no question, of course, of Our Savior being cleansed by the baptismal waters. St. Ambrose reflects on the event and says it was the other way 'round. Christ was baptized that He might cleanse the waters, that these might be washed by the flesh of Christ which knew not sin, and that He might so leave these waters sanctified for those later to be baptized. Moreover, says Chrysostom, Christ was no sinner that He Himself should have need of baptism. But He is the Incarnate Word. As man He has a nature that is sinful, a nature which, as it is in the rest of us, cries for the baptismal cleansing. St. Augustine, lastly, finds the reason for Our Savior's baptism in a matter of example. "He willed to do what He commanded others to do." For the eternal salvation of His faithful,

---

[1]*Summa Theologiae*, IIIa, q. 39.

baptism would be indispensable; by bowing His own head to the waters, He would demonstrate that necessity.

Not without reason, John hesitated to baptize Christ. He realized full well that it is for the servant to be baptized by the master, the creature by the Creator. But justice requires this, said Our Lord, and John complied. St. Matthew recounts the portents that followed. The heavens were opened to Him; the Holy Spirit descended in the form of a dove; the Father's voice was heard: "This is my beloved Son, in whom I am well pleased."

St. Thomas inquires about the reason for these portents, one and all. He finds such a reason in this principle: since Christ's baptism was the exemplar of our own, there ought to be manifested in it all that is actually accomplished in our own.

The heavens appeared as open to the Lord Christ — with reason, since it is through baptism that heaven's entrance is opened to us, His rational creatures. The Holy Spirit descended in the form of a dove, a real dove, notes St. Thomas, a dove whose presence signified the influence there present of the Holy Spirit as the fire signified the presence of God in the burning bush. Rightly did the Holy Ghost so appear, since the baptized with the baptism of Christ, in a real, objective way, do receive the Holy Spirit, together with all His coming entails — His gifts, for instance, and His fruits.

The voice of the Father was heard: "This is my beloved Son, in whom I am well pleased." Herein also is a sign of our own baptism. Extend the meaning of the word "son," and what holds true of Christ holds true of those baptized in Christ. For we are born again as adoptive sons of God. The adoptive son is not the natural son, but he is not a servant either, nor a distant relative, nor a weekend guest. "Those He foreknew," says St. Paul to the Romans, "He predestined to become conformed to the image of His Son."[2] In those so conformed, too, the eternal Father has reason to be well pleased.

All three Persons are present in the baptismal scene: the Son Incarnate, the Holy Spirit in the presence of the dove, the Father in the voice offering testimony. In this presence of the Triune God is manifested,

2Rom 8:29.

lastly, that our baptism is to be consecrated by the invocation and power of the Trinity. "Go forth and teach all nations" were Our Savior's last instructions, "baptizing them in the name of the Father, and of the Son, and of the Holy Spirit."[3]

In this day's Mass, the Church reminds us of Our Savior's baptism and thus indirectly recalls to us the reality of our own. It is not just an initiation rite into Christ's Church, this baptism of ours, nor the mere celebration of a name newly bestowed. It is a sacrament with effects that are enduring and operative, distinguishing and transforming. The descent of the Holy Spirit, heavens open to the vision of Christ, the Father's voice — these signify such effects and the difference they make and remind us thereof.

This same sacrament and the elevation it confers are not without their corresponding demands. The heavens were opened, says St. Luke in his account, while Christ was at prayer. St. Thomas reflects that this conjunction is not without its significance. For the baptized in Christ has need of *jugis oratio*, persevering prayer for the rest of his days, *ad hoc coelum introeat*, so that he might enter heaven, for there remain after baptism that weakened and wounded nature that compels to evil from within, the "world" and the devil that attack from without. "Jesus … ascended from the water," says St. Matthew. For the baptized, even this is not without meaning. St. Thomas reflects that ascent implies difficulty — as does the doing of good works, which needs must complement the baptism; and this means continuing and persevering effort. "Now that you have been buried with Christ through baptism, you have been raised with Him," says Paul. "If then you were raised with Christ, seek the things that are above."[4]

In the prayer of today's Mass, the Church combines admirably both the exemplar and its effects when we beg God, "When Christ was baptized in the Jordan, and the Holy Spirit descended upon Him, you didst solemnly declare Him your beloved Son; grant to the sons of your adoption, born of water and the Holy Spirit, that they may continually persevere in your good pleasure."

---

[3]Mt 28:19.   [4]cf. Col 2:12; 3:1.

13

SECOND SUNDAY AFTER EPIPHANY

(SECOND SUNDAY OF THE YEAR)

CANA

(Year C; John 2:1–11)

"A marriage took place at Cana of Galilee and the mother of Jesus was there. Now, Jesus, too, was invited … to the marriage."

Our Divine Lord at the wedding party found Himself in a situation in which most of us, I suppose, find ourselves from time to time. He belonged to no family. "I have come that they may have life and have it more abundantly."[1] "I am sent to the lost sheep of the house of Israel."[2] He came to work for three years before His sacrificial and redemptive death. His work was teaching for the most part — scattering the good seed everywhere, on good ground and on bad. This sower's work kept Him on the road. It meant for Him the sacrifice of family life. Having not "whereon to lay His head,"[3] He belonged to no human family.

The folks at Cana invited His mother to come, and Him and His disciples. For His own reasons He accepted. He spent this day — as He did others in the course of His life with the Lazarus clan — sharing in the warmth of a family.

Sometimes, I suppose, we find ourselves in a similar situation. Perhaps then we cannot help but feel a bit envious of this family whose kindness welcomes us. Let this simple fact embarrass no one. It is the natural power and destiny of any human being to love a husband or wife, to love one's own children, and be in turn loved and respected by them — to be important, to matter to someone.

This power and destiny we yield freely, but not without pain. Not without bitter struggle. We yield it in the interests of another, a greater, a

[1]Jn 10:10. [2]Mt 15:24. [3]Mt 8:20.

better but less tangible love. Is there any cause why we should not feel a certain stab of loss when, on occasion, we intercept the warm, eloquent look that passes between husband and wife? When, above all, we catch a glimpse of what it is for parents to be loved by their children?

This natural destiny with its joys, and of course its sorrows, too, about which we have said nothing, but which we know can sometimes bring anguished tears and crush the human spirit, was all implicit there at that wedding feast at Cana. Our Lord was there; but all that the day implied He had foresworn. Like our Master before us, and for the same reason, we too have foresworn it. Yet nonetheless, we are not solitary. Everyone calls us "father" or "sister." God's family is the Church, and in this exalted and holy family we have a place. A work of supernatural paternity or supernatural sisterliness is expected of us. What we have foresworn we have foresworn for the same goals Christ, Our Lord, came on earth to accomplish. As He did, let us not lament the loss; let us get on with the work. If, in turn, the fruitfulness of our lives for ourselves and others will prove to make this sacrifice of human love worthwhile, it will only be because our love of the Master has been so deep and so persevering as to be enough for us.

14

SECOND SUNDAY AFTER EPIPHANY
(SECOND SUNDAY OF THE YEAR)
CANA (2)

(Year C; John 2:1–11)

The marriage at Cana in Galilee which St. John sketches for us is one of those few events narrated in the Gospels that offer us a glimpse into the heart of the Blessed Mother of Christ. In the marvel that there took place and to which St. John refers as "this beginning of miracles," she played a key role. For she it was who, by her intercession with her Son, was the occasion thereof.

"They have no wine." St. Thomas reflects on these few words and remarks that in them shine forth the *pietas* and the *misericordia* of the Mother of God.[1] Hers is a devotion, a loyalty to her friends, to her acquaintances, that can be counted upon; it is a loyalty and devotion that did not fail there at Cana but moved her to do what she could. Hers is a devotion that never fails.

The few words she said came from a heart filled with mercy. St. Thomas reflects a bit on the derivation of this word *misericors* which we hear so often in the Latin liturgy. The adjective *miser* is familiar enough. *Cor, cordis* is "heart," and the merciful is he or she whose heart is wretched over the sorrows of another.

There is nothing more beautiful under heaven than the person so unselfish that he, or she, can so actually take to heart the woes of another as to make them his own. It is like becoming that other, the *alter ego*. "Which of you is ill, and I am not ill?" Paul asks of the Corinthians.[2] Such a rare person is the Mother of God. The embarrassment, the distress of her hosts, becomes her embarrassment, her distress.

---

[1] *Commentary on the Gospel of John*, c. 2, lect. 1.   [2] 2 Cor 11:29.

"They have no wine." Evidently she saw need to say no more than that. For her Divine Son she had no directions, no advice, no suggestions, no hints as to what particular measures He might take. Her *reverentia,* says St. Thomas, her respect for her Son is such that these measures she knows she can leave to His discretion, His kindness.

We would pray in much the same fashion, most likely, were our own reverence and respect for the wisdom and goodness of God modeled on hers. It should suffice us simply to present to Him our every want and defect. So prayed King David: "O Lord, before You is my every desire."[3] What precise ways and means the Lord God might select best to fulfill these needs — this we might be wise to leave up to Him.

This prayer of Our Lady's suggests the prayers of the Church which we read regularly as part of the Mass. Her prayer is, in a way, reflected in them. For the Church's petitions tend to be very general, rather than particular. One reason for this, of course, is the fact that the Mass prayer is supposed to be a summation of the petitions of all the faithful there present. But there is another reason. From the Church's prayers we can learn a little something about what it is best to ask for. I can ask God for health or wealth or even for a five horse parlay, at least to show. And all this is good. But what the Church's prayer suggests is that we need to keep in mind that God in His infinite wisdom really knows, far better than we do, where our true good lies. It is this that Providence envisages and aims at, and His plan never fails. Perhaps, consequently, it would be better to leave all the details to God and simply to move our hearts and lips in tune with the deep wisdom of the Mother of Christ: "They have no wine."

Or on the same model, the prayer of the moment would be: "There are exams this week."

Our Savior answered His mother, and His reply is mysterious enough: "What is it to me or to thee?" But the fact still remains that when His mother speaks, He listens. To relieve, at her request, the distress of His hosts, to establish, moreover, His credentials as one having authority because sent by God, the Lord Christ showed Himself the Master of Creation. His power reaches to the very natures of things. There were

[3] Ps 38:9.

six stone jugs standing by; He had them filled with water; that water He changed to wine.

"Bring this to the maitre d'," He instructs, and "Have him taste it." Chrysostom remarks that in His miracles, whatever the Lord Christ did, He did perfectly. His cure of Peter's mother-in-law was so quick and absolute that she rose immediately and waited on them. He restored the paralytic to such perfect health that the man was able to carry his own bed into his own house.[4]

Here also in the first of His miracles, says St. Thomas, it was no common wine that the Lord *de aqua fecit*, made from water, but the *optimum quod poterat esse* — the best that could be.

The miracle was not without its profound effect on the disciples of Christ. "His disciples believed in Him," says St. John. Peter and Andrew, John and Philip and Nathanial — these at least had been with Him for some days now. How they regarded Him previously, what drew them originally to Him, what it was in Him that bound them to Himself is not all that clear. Resting firmly on faith, our imagination would tell us that it was His godliness of manner — He was a gentleman — and the unquestionable authority with which He spoke.

But the miracle made a difference. They saw water made wine at His word; what they saw moved them. "His disciples believed in Him." St. John does not elaborate on precisely what he means by this. Whether there and then they realized His divinity is not all that clear.

One day the Savior put to them that question which all must at length confront: "Who do you say that I am?" By this miracle, evidently, were at least implanted in them the seeds of that mind which would move Peter, speaking for them all, to answer, "Thou art the Christ, the Son of the living God," and "Lord, to whom shall we go? Thou alone hast the words of eternal life."[5]

[4]Mk 1:31; Mk 2:12.   [5]Mt 16:15–16; Jn 6:68.

15

FOURTH SUNDAY AFTER EPIPHANY

(Matthew 8:23–27)

"But Jesus said to them, 'Why are you faint-hearted, men of little faith?' Then He rose up, and checked the winds and the sea, and there was deep calm."

The inspired evangelical portrait of Christ shows us a man, whoever and whatever else He was, performing deeds; and those deeds range from the most ordinary, like eating and sleeping, to the most stupendous, like raising the dead to life. In addition the Gospels leave no doubt that this man was possessed of certain unalterable interior convictions. These deep persuasions reveal themselves both in the personal actions of the man and in the demands He made, and made uncompromisingly, of those who would be associated with Him.

One such conviction in Christ was, clearly enough, the urgent need for fraternal love and, particularly, sincere forgiveness among men. Another of his preoccupations was the necessity of supernatural faith.

"Faith" is a word of double significance. Primarily faith means that intellectual process whereby a man assents to, or accepts as true, a given proposition, not because he himself sees evidence for it, but strictly on the word of someone else who vouches for the proposition. If the authority is God, the faith is supernatural.

Evidently though, the faith which Christ in the Gospels kept demanding is different from this act of simple credence. In this other meaning, faith means confidence, firm trust, unqualified reliance on Almighty God in every contingency. Our Savior repeatedly reproached

His followers for deficiency in such confidence; indeed, no single repre-hension falls more freely from the lips of Christ than this: "Why are you faint-hearted, men of little faith?" One hears in that pained question the very tones of Christ, tones of mystification and exasperation. He simply cannot comprehend why anyone who is granted any knowledge of God's power and God's love can doubt for an instant that loving power and powerful love.

Nor can we escape the Christian obligation to absolute trust in God by pleading that, at the moment, all appearances militate against it. When the Lord Christ uttered the protest just now quoted, He had to raise His voice against the uproar of a vicious lake storm that threatened momentarily to overturn the creaking, heaving skiff in which He and the disciples were perched.

Every syllable of these remarks on faith as confidence has been uttered, and frequently, before. Yet all must be said again. A world of interior peace, as well as a warmer, more cordial relationship with God, is waiting for every one of us who finally resolves to give to Christ, Our Lord, against all appearances, the big, strong, steady faith that He asks.

16

FOURTH SUNDAY AFTER EPIPHANY (2)

(Matthew 8:23–27)

Christ, Our Lord, was a prey to incidentals. He was a victim of incessant annoyances which left Him no peace. He could never carry out without interruptions what He planned to do.

He was so dead tired that He slept even in a small boat, bounced about by the storm-whipped waves on the lake. Even then the Apostles could not let Him be. In their terror they shook Him and screamed at Him, "Lord, save us! We perish!"

Another time He sits down to dinner at Simon's house, and Magdalene comes and interrupts Him. While He is deliberately discussing religion with the Pharisees at home, He is distracted by a paralytic let down through a hole in the roof. He comes down from a night in the hills to address the people and is stopped by a leper. They all want something from Him. He is moving southward from the lake, and His path is crossed by the cortege of the son of the widow from Naim. He is tired and thirsty; He walks to Jacob's well for a drink of cool water and finds Himself engaged in a lengthy discussion of morals with a schismatic woman. He passes from Cana to Nazareth, and the official breaks in on Him: "Speak but the word and my son will be healed." He goes on what seems to be a bit of a vacation along the coast of Tyre, and the Syro-Phoenician breaks in on His retirement and makes His presence known. To these people in this place He was not sent. He does not come to them, but they come to Him.[1]

---

[1]Lk 7:38; Lk 5:19; Mt 8:2; Lk 7:12; Jn 4:6; cf. Jn 4:47/Mt 8:5; Mk 7:25.

Accidental encounters all. To some extent this catalogue of events reminds us of any one of our own days. It is our vocation to follow the Master as a teacher — in a public life — being available to the crowds. Sometimes you find you cannot walk from one building to another, from one end of a corridor to another, without being approached, addressed, interrupted, beseeched. They all want something from you, and it is their convenience they consult, not yours. You can't sit down for a minute's rest but some student interrupts. If not in person, there is always the phone.

The Apostles did not always see these myriad interruptions as part of the scheme of things. Sometimes they tried to interfere, as when they endeavored to chase the children.[2] Sometimes they were simply bewildered, as in Samaria when they found Him engaged with the woman at the well. Sometimes they were exasperated, or even frightened, as with the Syro-Phoenician woman. For the most part they were simply acquiescent, knowing His interest in the people.

At best they looked upon such incidental events as interruptions — unpredictable, accidental, pointless. Pretty much the same as we consider interruptions in our day which eat up precious time, destroy our planning, try our patience, arouse irritations and tensions, even bewilder us because of a lack of rhyme or reason.

Perhaps it is a bit of blindness on our part to interpret our day in just this way. The myriad incidental events are chance and accidental only to our human eyes. God in His providence pulls all the threads and all the strings. In His eyes they all are for a purpose — some good known to Himself.

In Our Lord's case a tremendous love and a deep and genuine interest in every human being drove Him forward. He was never off-duty. What good can be done? Here and now? This was not included in my plans, but nonetheless here it is. It is an opportunity.

Our own set order in each day is like Simon's invitation to Our Lord. It assures our presence at a given spot at a given time. All else God Himself arranges for purposes we know not, except that in some way they have to do with the good of souls — mine and others. What to us in our narrowness of vision may seem but a casual, passing meeting may

---

[2]Mt 19:13

register in His limitless vision as the turning point in the salvation of a soul. He sees the whole picture, and in the whole picture is the "why" of it. If at times we are bewildered, exasperated, wearied, the reason lies in our inability to see. But it is unnecessary for us to know the why of things, only the fact that presents itself inescapably. This is our task — to rise above the annoyance of the moment and try to turn this to some good for the kingdom.

LENT

17

SUNDAY BEFORE LENT

This coming Wednesday is Ash Wednesday, and the violet vestments will make their appearance once again on the altar. When this happens at the beginning of Lent, what shocks us a bit as season melts into season, liturgical hope into liturgical sorrow, is the realization that time and mortal life are slipping away with indecent celerity.

What is salutary is not to waste time in idle regrets over what is past and done with, but to calculate anew how the time that remains, whether much or little, shall be used to best advantage.

St. Paul, as the lad Saul in Tarsus, intently watched the athletes compete in the stadium. Later he told his Christians at Corinth, and through them, us, that when men run a race, the race is for all, but the prize is for one. True enough; and there is no one of us but wants to be a winner in this, the only mortal life we will ever have. But how does one run "for victory"? The voice of the Apostle comes ringing down to us. "Every athlete," he says, "must keep his appetites under control."[1]

This is indeed a perverse moral and social climate in which we live. Our day and age knows and admits that, in any number of connections, "every athlete must keep his appetites under control." The anachronistic prize-fighter, the ever-hungry jockey, the professional dancer, the perfectly disciplined astronaut, even the stout fellow threatened with an early exit because of too many entrées: of all these it is demanded that they face the harsh facts of life and simply "bring those appetites under control."

---

[1] 1 Cor 9:25.

But in the name of an enlightened age, don't encourage children to do without sweets for a religious motive; don't ask people to fast and abstain in quiet memory of the passion of Christ; don't suppose it wise or constructive that a man eschew alcohol or tobacco in reparation to the Sacred Heart. If the appetites are to be brought under control, says our day, this makes sense if it is to win a crown that perishes, but not if it is to win a crown that is imperishable.

"All things have their season," says Ecclesiastes.[2] "There is a time for fasting," says the Church of Christ, "and this is it." The Church has always taken seriously Paul's admonition to the Corinthians. Over the centuries, with a wisdom born of the Holy Spirit, she has recognized and appreciated the sound psychology implicit therein.

Sensible pleasure is just that — pleasure. By definition it is what all animals, including those of the rational variety, naturally want. Just as naturally they deplore its contrary.

But Adam's sin deprived us of the gifts of God that stabilized the right order of things. His sin turned us topsy-turvy, so to speak. The punishment of his sin is a disorder born into our very nature. Instead of a good in its own proper place in the right order of things, pleasure has established itself in the tyrant's place. It is now our greatest source of temptation, and in that sense the unhappy truth is that our own flesh is our worst enemy. "No pestilence is more efficacious for the doing of mischief," says Boethius, "than the enemy that's closest to us,"[3] and we read in the Book of Wisdom, "The corruptible body is a load upon the soul."[4]

The result is a kind of slavery that we have to free ourselves from and struggle against with the help of God's grace. "For I know that there dwelleth not in me, that is to say in my flesh, that which is good. For to will is present to me; but to accomplish that which is good I find not. For the good which I will, I do not; but the evil which I will not, that I do."[5] So St. Paul confessed to the Romans. We need, by continued effort, to break free.

To extinguish the lower appetites would be neither desirable nor possible, and the Apostle speaks of no such extinction. He says, "They

[2]Eccl 3:1.   [3]cf. *The Three Greatest Prayers*, p. 151.   [4]Wis 9:15.   [5]Rom 7:18–19.

must be controlled." No one comes by such control by a mere *fiat* of a good will; no single resolution, however firm, will by itself do the trick.

Virtue is a habit, and the virtue here required is temperance. Habits don't come about except through repeated acts. During Lent the Church wants no one to undertake anything that would in any way or to any degree injure health, impair vigor, or diminish efficiency. But she does urge, over a period of time, some self-denial of the sweets and the repose that please but aren't all that necessary; the undertaking of some work beyond what is demanded, good in itself, entailing the challenge of some difficulty.

There is a point to the Church's commendation; the psychology is sound, and it is our own good in the shape of a firm moral backbone that is envisaged. When the grosser sins threaten to throw us as we hustle along the way of salvation, when ease and pleasure make us shy away from the challenge implicit in a higher grace, then it is possible, perhaps even easy and quasi-natural, to resist if we have denied our natural cravings previously and done it more than once. What we have done, we can do, and what once bordered on the impossible becomes easier through repetition. The Church would have self-mastery become a part of us. Therefore she commends some self-denial freely undertaken and persevered in, and therefore Lent.

This season approaches. Generally it strikes our imagination as grim and gray, the closest approximation on this earth to the actually infinite. But it is a liturgical season based on sound psychology, necessary with the necessity of the conditional variety. St. Paul, himself such a superb athlete of Christ, clarifies for us that condition: we must deny ourselves, yes, if we are to win the race.

18

FIRST SUNDAY OF LENT

TEMPTATION

(Year A; Genesis 2:7–9; 3:1–7; Matthew 4:1–11; Luke 4:1–13)

The Old Testament selection of this first Sunday of Lent, and the Gospel narrative as well, remind us most forcefully of the grim reality of him to whom we refer as the Prince of Darkness, whom Our Savior named the Prince of this world, that leering reality that lurks behind all evil, finally: the implacable fallen angel who will not give over his plan to poison all that is good, the invisible malice who, if he could delight, would delight that men no longer believe in him.

But St. Peter, for instance, in his first epistle is insistent on Satan's reality, the reality of his being and the reality of his hatred: "Your adversary goes about like a roaring lion seeking whom he may devour."[1] And St. Paul calls the Ephesians to vigilance by reminding them that "our struggle is against principalities and powers, against the rulers of this world's darkness."[2]

In the course of his explanation of the Lord's prayer, St. Thomas addresses himself to the petition "Lead us not into temptation."[3] He sees temptation as coming from three sides — the flesh, the devil, and the world. The temptation of the flesh, he tells us, is *valde gravis*, serious indeed, because it is the flesh of our own fallen nature that is the foe, and it is conjoined to us, part of us. It is our own selves that clamor for pleasure. But there is no enemy more damaging, says Boethius, than the *familiaris inimicus*, the enemy of one's own household. "Watch and pray," therefore Our Redeemer warns us, "that you enter not into temptation."[4]

---

[1] 1 Pet 5:8.   [2] Eph 6:12.   [3] *Opuscula Theologica, In Orationem Dominicam Expositio*; cf. *The Three Greatest Prayers.*   [4] Mt 26:41.

After the flesh has been trampled underfoot — *conculcatur* — continues St. Thomas, then the second enemy moves in, the devil. If this is so, then Satan actually need concern himself but little, if at all, with the bulk of men: they never reach that condition. Their own concupiscence is never brought to heel, and it remains always sufficient to keep them in the enemy's camp; no incitement from him is necessary.

But then when Satan does approach, he does so, the theologian continues, most cleverly, like a sagacious general besieging a fort. He looks for the weak points and moves against them. In the case of the temperate, these are most likely to be contemptuousness and vanity and pride.

In any case this day's Gospel narrative makes it abundantly clear that not without truth did C.S. Lewis write *The Screwtape Letters*. Although he can well leave the crowd to their own greed and unbridled concupiscence, still Satan does find individuals worth his attention. He must, of course, keep an attentive eye on the brains and muscle of society — the legislators and the courts, the moguls of the media, and above all, the educators. It is no small achievement for him that, on the grand scale, evil should be unquestioningly accepted as the norm. Be that as it may, what appears clear from this day's readings is that his diabolical cunning is directed also at the best and the holiest, at Eve, for instance, in whom the grace of God abounded, and at the Incarnate Word of God Himself. "It is on the sanctified," says Hilary, "that the temptations of the devil lie heaviest, for it is victory over the holy that he desires most."

Should the evil one approach, how not to deal with him we can best learn from Eve. She delayed; she entertained the proffered motion; she discussed and debated the issue. She lost. The God-man, on the contrary, dallies not, nor does He discuss nor debate; He bargains not, nor does He compromise. "Not on bread alone does man live … Thou shalt do homage to the Lord, thy God, Him alone shalt thou adore … Thou shalt not tempt the Lord, thy God." He is sharp, prompt, firm, determined, strong, absolute, final.

In his Tertia Pars, St. Thomas has written a four-article question on the temptation of Christ.[5] The second of these articles focuses on the

---

[5] IIIa, q. 41.

place of the temptation. Why the desert? What is it that is appropriate about the wasteland as the site of temptation?

The Lord Christ of course could not be tempted from within, as we can, for such temptation implies subjection to sin in one way or another. Yet He did offer Himself to be tempted by Satan and offered Himself of His own free will and choice, just as later He would offer Himself of His own free will to Satan and his minions to be slain. Otherwise the devil would not have dared to approach Him. But the devil is more apt to approach the good person when he is solitary. Hence Our Redeemer went out alone into the desert and, St. Thomas adds, as to a battlefield, to challenge the devil; to dare him; to invite, as it were, his temptations, that by struggling with him He might conquer him.

As we say, in all that the Lord Christ did, He is an example to His followers. In view of this, one might just wonder at the prudence of this particular venture. Is it to be judged salutary for Christ's followers that they should so challenge angelic cunning? Such a procedure might just appear temerarious at best and foolish at worst.

This little problem does not escape the theologian, and he replies to it in one of his responses. To invite temptations has two senses. There is the familiar sense, and it comes to mind first — rashly to put oneself in what we have long called an occasion of sin. This is indeed one way to challenge the devil, and in it there is nothing prudent, commendable, or salutary. As the Lord God said to Lot: "Don't dally in the vicinity of Sodom."[6] What temptation results from such a situation, the tempted himself has asked for. He has brought it on himself and has already done wrong in placing himself in such a situation.

But there is another meaning to the phrase "to invite temptation." Take the Christian life seriously, the life dedicated to virtue and holiness and to the imitation of Christ. Venture upon it, strive to adhere to it and to progress therein, and this is to challenge the devil. For "*semper invidet ad meliora tendentibus*," says St. Ambrose. "He has his envious eye on those who strive for better things."

---

[6] cf. Gen 19:17–22.

St. John Chrysostom explains in his own commentary on Matthew:

> Not only was Christ led into the desert by the Spirit, but so also
> are all the sons of God who possess that same Holy Spirit, for they
> are not content to sit idle, but the Holy Spirit moves them to take
> hold of some great work. But the world of good works, in Satan's
> eyes, is the desert; the world of goodness is a barren land, for there
> is nothing there in which Satan can take delight.

To live as a sincere follower of Christ is so to enter into the desert, to challenge Satan, and to invite his forays.

This, says St. Thomas, *non est periculosum*. No danger here, not because the adopted son of God puts his trust in his own spiritual strength — he doesn't — but because it is the Holy Spirit who is the author and inspirer of the perfect work, and the assistance of His grace is stronger than the attacking force of the enemy who detests that good work.

When the devil had finished all this tempting, angels came and ministered to Christ. And, adds St. Luke in his account, the devil "left Him, to await another opportunity." That opportunity came, evidently, on the first Holy Thursday and Good Friday when the Lord offered Himself again to the fury of the Prince of Darkness and his hordes. On that occasion Satan won and, in winning, was vanquished forever.

19

SECOND SUNDAY OF LENT

TRANSFIGURATION

(Year A; Genesis 12:1–4; Matthew 17:1–9; Mark 9:2–10; Luke 9:28–36)

Generally the first reading of the Sunday Mass is linked to the Gospel selection. The two readings combine to focus our attention on some one theme and remind us of some single lesson. This Sunday's Mass is no exception, although that lesson is perhaps more obscure than often. The first reading recalls Abraham, and God's command to pack up, leave his native Ur of the Chaldees, and cross the miles of desert to "the land I will show you." The Gospel selection narrates Our Savior's transfiguration. Disparate as these two incidents are, a common lesson does emerge, and in view of that lesson we might just re-christen this second Sunday of Lent "Hope Sunday," or "A Reason for Hope Sunday."

What the Lord God enjoined on Abraham was, clearly enough, a project of major magnitude: an uprooting of himself, his family, his stock, and his things; a journey of no small distance across trackless wastes to an unfamiliar land. What God bade him undertake was in fact the sort of trek that our own green land witnessed time and again more than a century ago when so many Americans packed their families and belongings in Conestoga wagons or prairie schooners, bade farewell to their dear ones, and set out from St. Louis or Omaha across the prairie and the mountains and the deserts beyond.

No one undertakes hardship of such a sort, and no one lays himself open to ever-threatening danger, without hope of a good, proportionate to the difficulties undertaken; no one perseveres without such hope. Our forebears hoped for freedom and security somewhere along the Santa Fe or Oregon Trails, or for sudden wealth in the Mother Lode country. God Himself made unmistakably clear to the aged Abraham what it was he had to hope for, the boon that was to be his at the end of his trek: "I will make your nation great, and I will bless you; I will make your name great so that you will be a blessing." Abraham believed and, with hope for that inestimable good, "went where the Lord directed him."

Matthew, Mark, Luke — all three recount the mystery in the life of Our Savior which we read just a few moments ago and to which we refer as His transfiguration.

It was the last year of His life. The Lord Christ was in Jerusalem for the feast of the Tabernacles. He was there to mingle among the crowds as the Good Shepherd to seek out His lost sheep, to teach the willing the saving truth He had come to teach.

The Tabernacles was a week-long feast, and on the sixth day, says St. Matthew, Christ called to Himself Peter, James, and John. He led them out of the city. Together they climbed one of the higher hills about the town. On the summit thereof He was transfigured before them.

The Evangelists are brief, sketchy in their account of this transfiguration. It is as if what dazzled the eyes of three chosen Apostles was beyond the power of their human words to describe. The Evangelists offer only a few phrases. "He was transfigured: His clothes became dazzlingly white, whiter than any earthly bleacher could make them." "He was transfigured," relates St. Matthew, "His face shone like the sun and His clothes became as white as the light." And St. Luke: "The appearance of His face was changed, and His clothing became as brilliant as lightning." He remained recognizably Himself, but it was as if His Divine nature shone through. The Apostles saw and were afraid, for "who can look upon God and live?"

We might just wonder about the purpose of Our Savior's transfiguration — why was He transfigured before these Apostles, and why at this particular time? — and it might just be the case that we find the key in the sequence of events.

St. Thomas, in the Tertia Pars, devotes a four-article question to this transfiguration of Christ.[1] In the first of these articles, he asks

---

[1] IIIa, q. 45.

"Whether it was fitting that Christ have been transfigured." He answers the question by resolving the mystery into its final cause — the why.

Here the sequence of events assumes no little importance. In all three Gospel accounts, the transfiguration of Jesus of Nazareth follows closely His first detailed prediction of His passion. "It is necessary that the Son of Man should suffer many things, and be rejected by the elders, and the chief priests and the scribes, and be put to death, and on the third day arise again" — words, those, that must needs have shocked, saddened, horrified, and mystified His chosen twelve. Soon in fact the Apostles would see their beloved leader rise to within sight and sound of stunning victory, only to be finally vanquished. They would see Him betrayed and flogged, crowned with thorns and broken upon the cross. They would see Him crushed with the finality of death.

So, says St. Thomas, "*Praenuntiata sua passione, induxerat eos ad suae passionis sequelam.*" Now that He had confided to them His passion to come, this prediction He follows with a preview to three of them, a preview of the glory that would follow that passion.

Our Savior forewarns His twelve of the agony and failure that lie before Him whom they had left all to follow. Then He is gloriously transfigured before them. St. Thomas reflects on this sequence and universalizes: If we are going to persevere on the road, then we must have some idea, at least, of the goal that lies ahead. If this is generally true, it is all the truer when the "*via est difficilis et aspera, et iter laboriosum, finis vero iucundus,*" when the way is difficult and rough, harsh, and the journey laborious, but the end truly delightful. When times are black and the situation grave, when the call is for perseverance, self-denial, and courage, when the horizon offers nothing but opposition and failure, it is not in the nature of us human creatures to persevere unless we have a pretty fair idea of what the goal of all this is. Moreover, we need a solid conviction that this goal is well worth the pain required to achieve it.

During these black, despairing, and uncertain days of the passion to come, three at least of His Apostles, leaders among them, would cherish a vision to keep their hopes alive. The memory of Christ gloriously transfigured before their eyes would be a blazing intimation of the glory that would finally be His when the passion would be over and He would be risen from the dead, the ultimate victor forever.

St. Thomas reflects also on this glory of Christ's previewed on the mountain, His eternally. He remarks: "And to this same end He brings also those who follow the footsteps of His passion." "If any man would be my disciple, let him take up his cross daily and come, follow me,"[2] but the goal of it all is to be the same for the disciple as for the Master. "The risen Christ," says St. Paul, "is the first fruits of those who have fallen asleep."[3] Again, he informs the Philippians, and through them, us: "From heaven will come the Lord Jesus Christ, and He will transform these wretched bodies of ours into images of His own glorious body."[4] What three Apostles beheld on the mountain is what we are all intended eventually to be.

Today we are approaching the middle of Lent. In the heart of this penitential season, the Church summons us to reawaken our appreciation of the unspeakable grandeur that lies ahead. Abraham set out and persevered in the hope of a great good promised. Remembrance of the glory they beheld on the mountain encouraged three Apostles to persevere; let reflection on the same do the same for us.

---

[2]Mk 8:34.   [3]1 Cor 15:20.   [4]cf. Phil 3:20–21.

20

THIRD SUNDAY OF LENT

SAMARITAN WOMAN

(Year A; Exodus 17:3–7; John 4:5–42)

Alife passed in this southwestern part of these United States seems to carry with it a deeper understanding and appreciation of Scripture's frequent references to water, a sympathetic understanding that one might never acquire, for instance, in the green East where lakes and flowing rivers abound. One who has lived through our recent weeks here might indeed be reluctant to believe it, but the fact remains that this is an arid corner of God's world. And Palestine would appear to have been much the same — a land of deserts and dry stream beds where every drop of water was precious, no one took it for granted, and the supply thereof was jealously guarded.

Two of the scriptural passages we have just read center about water. In the Old Testament selection we read of Moses in the wilderness about Meribah. At God's command, he struck the rock of Horeb and provided his thirsty and complaining thousands with not just a pool, but a continuous and fresh flow of that vital element without which life cannot exist.

In the Gospel narrative we catch a glimpse, first of all, of the kind of life Our Savior daily led. His was never a moment that He could call His own. We can believe St. John when he reports that the Lord Christ was "wearied from His journey," and we might just accordingly wish Him a few moments of restful solitude seated there on the low rock wall that rimmed Jacob's well. But it was not to be; we glean here and there from the Gospels that it rarely, if ever, was to be. In this instance, there was a woman who approached from the direction of Sichem, her water jug on her head. She filled her jug and turned to depart. Our Savior could have given Himself to the peaceful solitude of His own prayerful thoughts. But this was one of the ill who needed the attentions of the doctor. So the signs of weariness vanished from the Divine Physician's face. Moved by that love that motivated His every moment, He took the initiative: "Give me to drink."

Gently, masterfully, He led her from the familiar to the totally unknown. From a few words about the water she had come to draw from the well, He turned her thoughts to water of quite another sort, of whose existence she had never guessed, water simply vital because vital for eternity. He gave her an intimation, moreover, that this was no ordinary Jew with whom she conversed, but one of supreme importance and the giver of that very water of which He spoke. Before His Apostles' return from town, He had led her to a confrontation with the disorder of her own life, a first step, perhaps, on the road to godliness. He led her to an act of faith. "Thou art a prophet," she said to Him, and to her fellow townsfolk later: "He revealed to me all that I did; can not He be the Messiah?" And "Many of the townspeople came to believe in Him through her."

"If you had known the gift of God," He said to her. She had no idea when she picked up her jug that particular day and walked toward the well — a daily chore, most likely — whom, in the providence of God, she would encounter there and the difference that this one visit to the well would make.

But the gift to which Our Savior referred was not primarily that — her chance encounter with Him that appears to have altered her life — but rather the living water itself that He came to give: that supernatural, transfiguring reality that we call sanctifying grace.

It is not without reason that Divine Wisdom uses the metaphors He does. If He refers to His grace as water it is because He sees similarities there, similarities in more than one effect, and those similarities He would have us note.

Consider water simply as a cleanser of ourselves and our things; we would be lost without it. But cleanser, too, is the grace of Christ, cleanser *par excellence*, for it washes away the stain of sin; it blots out the debt of eternal punishment due that sin. "I shall pour forth on you a new water," was Ezekiel's prophecy, "and you shall be cleansed from your sins."[1]

There is no one of us who does not know the welcome delight of cool water and the refreshment it offers from the summer heat — both internally and externally. In this way too, the grace of Christ is not without its similarity to water. Man has a way of speaking of his passions, lower appetites, in terms of fire, heat. But "water quenches a flaming fire," we read in Ecclesiasticus,[2] and where the grace of Christ resides, there the mind is wiser and the will firmer in the right. With the assistance of grace, and not without it, struggling man can bring the fires of the lower appetites under control, and the result is that inner tranquility of order that we call peace.

But water is primarily the blessing it is as the quencher of thirst. So too is grace, but with a difference, as Our Savior Himself intimates: "Everyone who drinks this water will thirst again; but whoever drinks of the water I shall give shall not thirst forever."

What Our Savior says is true enough: who drank that well water thirsted again. In this it resembles the baubles and trinkets that this world sets its heart on. When deluded man doesn't have them, they seem desirable. He yearns for them, labors for them, and finally makes them his own. But they have a way of disappointing. So man sets his heart on something else, and the same result occurs again, and again, and again. "They have all passed like a shadow," we read in the Book of Wisdom.[3]

It is God, finally, the infinite good, who is the good for whom our souls thirst. "My soul has thirsted for God, the living font," says the Psalmist.[4] But, says Our Savior, "Who drinks of the water I shall give shall not thirst forever." For His grace is no less than the beginning of eternal life; its final flowering is that Beatific Vision that writes *finis* to all thirst. "They will be filled with the richness of your house," says the Psalmist.[5] In the New Law, grace is justice, and in the Sermon on the Mount, Christ promises: "Blessed are those who hunger and thirst after justice, for they shall be filled."[6]

"He would give you living water" were Our Redeemer's words to the woman at the well. Living water would seem to be opposed to

---

[1]Ezek 36:25.   [2]Ecclus 3:30.   [3]Wis 5:9.   [4]Ps 42:2.   [5]Ps 36:8.   [6]Mt 5:6.

the stagnant. The latter is cut off from its source; it collects in pools and dries up. The living water remains continuous with its source and flows ever, like the font Moses provided at Horeb or, closer to home, like the marvelous springs at Ferndale. His grace is of that sort. It flows from the Holy Spirit as from its source and cause, and disposes the soul for the Spirit's own dwelling therein. "The charity of God is poured forth into our hearts," says St. Paul, "through the Holy Spirit, who is given to us."[7] Where grace is, its source is necessarily there with it — living water, inseparable from its source.

The events of the Old Testament are the types, the foreshadowings of the realities of the New. We read in today's first lesson of Moses striking the rock of Horeb, and we are beholding a figure of Christ: Christ who, by His agony and death willingly accepted out of obedience, would give the water that renews and beautifies the souls of men. His own soul was filled with that grace, and so He can be the unending source for us — a truth St. John is at pains ever to emphasize. "We saw His glory," he says in the prologue to his Gospel, "the glory of the only-begotten of the Father, full of grace and truth ... and of His fullness we have all received."[8]

---

[7]Rom 5:5.   [8]Jn 1:14, 16.

21

FOURTH SUNDAY OF LENT

MAN BORN BLIND

(Year A; Ephesians 5:8–14; John 9:1–41)

Evidently the man born blind sat each day there in the temple yard and begged for his sustenance. When he obeyed the instructions of Jesus of Nazareth, betook himself across town to the waters of Siloam, washed therein, and then suddenly discovered what it is to see, this must indeed have been the most glorious moment of his life. But as so often happens in this vale of tears, he found himself shortly embroiled in a public hassle, and then the subject of two painful grillings at the hands of the Pharisees.

One portion, at least, of those worthies appears bent on destroying Jesus of Nazareth. If they could not condemn Him for violation of the Sabbath, then they might bully the poor unfortunate into admission of complicity in some sort of fraud relating to the miracle, or into accusing Our Savior of some kind of devilry or witchcraft.

The man born blind is left nameless by St. John. But he is as sharply drawn as any character in the Gospel narratives. Throughout his ordeal, he comes through to us as a remarkable and an admirable man. He was a first-rate witness, for one thing, who adhered to the facts as he knew them, with no elaborations. "I went, I washed, and I saw." He was a man of discernment and honesty sufficient to recognize his benefactor for what He was. If confession of what he believed was unpopular in that company, no matter, he would affirm it nonetheless. "If this man is a sinner, how can He do works like this?" was his own honest question to his less honest questioners, and then when they asked him what he deemed the man called Jesus to be, there was no hesitation in his answer: "He is a prophet."

It is toward the end of his second grilling that his constancy becomes most admirable. The Pharisees pressured him by placing him under oath. "Give glory to God … " Then they stated their case so as to induce him to retract or change his story: "We know that this man is a sinner … We know that God spoke to Moses, but this man, we do not know where He is from." The man born blind stood firm. In fact he seems to have ridiculed them to their face as if nothing could be more evident than that Jesus of Nazareth was from God: "You don't know where He comes from," he exclaimed, "and yet He opened my eyes. We know that God does not hear sinners, but that if someone is devout and obeys His will, He listens to him. It is unheard of that anyone ever gave sight to a person blind from birth. If this man were not from God, He could never have done such a thing."

All that he said was true, and his words were no more than a clear statement of what should have been obvious to his tormentors, and what would have been except that none are so blind as those who will not see. But in exasperation they made their accusation first, "You were born in sin totally," and then implied presumption on his part: "Do you teach us?" Then abandoning reason altogether, they brought the case to a conclusion. Says St. John, "They threw him outside." St. Thomas Aquinas, in his commentary on this part of St. John's Gospel, remarks that in this they were guilty of a threefold sin — lying, pride, and injustice.[1]

"You were born in sin totally," they said, judging according to the standards of the Old Law, standards epitomized, for example, in the words of Eliphaz to the crushed and ruined Job: "Remember, I pray thee, whoever perished being innocent? Or when were the just destroyed? On the contrary I have seen those who work iniquity, and sow sorrows, and reap them, perishing by the blast of God, and consumed by the spirit of His wrath."[2]

It was the logic of the Old Law. The Apostles themselves were apparently still ruled by it, judging from the question they put to Our Savior when they first encountered the unfortunate in the temple yard.

---

[1]c. 9, lect. 3.   [2]Job 4:7–9.

He was born blind; this must have been owing to someone's sin. "You were born totally in sin," the Pharisees charged him, as if the sin involved infected his whole person, flowing over from his soul to infect even the eyes of his body. But the accusation was a slander, and for that we have Incarnate Wisdom's own testimony: "Neither this man sinned, nor his parents, but that the works of God may be manifest in him."

Here, too, Our Savior touches upon the only reason why God ever allows any evil, moral or physical, in this universe of ours — for the sake of some proportional good, whether that good is evident to us or not. In this case it was "that the works of God be manifest in Him." But it is through the works of God that God Himself is known, and this is a great good, the ultimate and supreme good finally.

"Do you teach us?" the Pharisees asked him. There was pride in these words, and arrogance. There was truth in all he said, but they would not listen because the words came from below their own exalted station. St. Thomas takes the occasion to remark that every man, no matter how wise he may be, ought not to reject *doctrinam*, learning, truth, *a quocumque parvo*, no matter how little the one from whom it comes.

In addition to their lie and their arrogance, they were guilty also of gross injustice. All their victim did was speak the truth, and from this he did not merit being cast out. Actually, in him was already fulfilled the benediction promised by Our Savior on the Mount: "Blessed are you when men will hate you and will persecute you and will cast out your name as evil because of the Son of Man."[3]

When word of this man's constancy and loyalty to Him, at no small cost to himself, reached Our Savior, He would not let such virtue go unrecognized and unsupported. He sought him out and found him finally. How different that countenance must have appeared now that the light of vision shone in those eyes. His beneficiary, too, gazed upon his benefactor for the first time. It becomes apparent here that the workings of Christ's grace within him had bestowed a second sight, higher and more precious than the first: the light of faith. "'I believe, Lord,'" he said, "and falling down, he adored Him."

Christ's words to the Pharisees, the closing words of the episode,

---

[3]Lk 6:22.

point to what must have been indeed one of the deepest and most endur-ing sufferings of His Sacred Heart. "I have come into this world unto judgment, that those who do not see may see, and that those who see may become blind."

Actually, so far as purpose is concerned, He came only for the first part: that those who did not see — the Gentiles — might in due time see. "Unto the people who walked in darkness there has shone a great light," prophesied Isaiah.[4] But, "This child is set for the ruin and resurrection of many in Israel," announced Simeon so many years before.[5] His com-ing became the occasion of willful, stubborn blindness on the part of His own people, stiff-necked unto the end. It is this same willful blind-ness that He charges the Pharisees with: "'We see,' you say, and your sin remains." "If I had not come," He said on another occasion, "they would not have sinned."[6] They preferred the darkness to the light. He came out of love to save the world, and as a result of His coming His own people were infinitely worse off than if He had not come at all.

As Jesus of Nazareth stood to the man born blind, so He stands to us all. "So long as I am in the world," He said, "I am the light of the world."[7] *Sol iustitiae*, the sun of justice, the prophet Malachi foretold Him.[8] He is our sun, in the light of whose teaching, and in the light of whose grace to see and understand that teaching, we direct our steps. "As long as I am in the world." From the time He spoke those words until His ascension, it was the world's joy to have Him visibly present in its midst. He is no longer so. Little matter, for He is still just as effectively present through the enlightening, transforming reality that we call His grace. "Behold, I am with you all days, even to the consummation of the world."[9]

The Apostle is insistent that the fact that Christ is our light has to make a difference in our lives. "The night has passed," he wrote to the Romans, "and the day will approach. Let us therefore put off the works of darkness and put on the armor of light."[10] To the Christians of Ephesus he says the same, in equally general terms, when he says as we heard just a short while ago, "Live as children of light. Light produces every kind of goodness and justice and truth." And he ends with the brief exhortation, "Awake, O sleeper, and arise from the dead, and Christ will give you light."

---

[4]Is 9:2.　[5]Lk 2:34.　[6]Jn 15:22.　[7]Jn 8:12.　[8]Mal 4:2.　[9]Mt 28:20.　[10]Rom 13:12.

22

FOURTH SUNDAY OF LENT (2)

PRODIGAL SON

(Year C; Luke 15:1–3, 11–32)

There are some who regard the tale we have just read as the pearl among Christ's parables. It is a story that wells up from the love of Our Savior's Sacred Heart; it is the masterpiece of the imagination of God. The parable appears as an almost desperate attempt to convey what the Incarnate Word understands and what His rational creatures can't begin to comprehend — the depths of God's boundless love for us.

The point of the narrative lies, clearly enough, in the contrast — the sharp and deep contrast — between the reception the younger son anticipated on his return home, and the welcome he actually received.

He hadn't behaved at all well toward his father. He requested his inheritance; he took it and quit his home for no good reason. In his own way he showed the older generation what he thought of them and the life they loved and led. When good parents suffer thus, it hurts.

With his money in his pocket, he set out for the merry life. Most likely the sensuous life began to cloy and pall, as it has a way of doing, in not too long a time. At any rate it proved expensive: "He squandered his money in dissolute living." As his money disappeared, so did his friends. At the bottom of his fortunes, he found himself alone, penniless, staving off actual starvation by sharing the fodder of animals.

In his desperation, sadder but wiser, he could see but one course open. He had to take his chances and return home. Not primarily to heal the hurt he had dealt his father, but rather to escape from his own present intolerable situation.

He envisions his own return, his chances of acceptance, the humiliation to which he would have to submit, the apologies and promises he would have to make. He would have to humble himself, seek out his father, wait upon his good pleasure, arrange an interview, make his apologies, ask for a job.

It doesn't happen that way. He is still afar off when he catches sight of his father running toward him as if the aged parent had been scanning the highway. Far from having to seek an interview, he finds himself embraced and kissed midst tears of joy. He offers his prepared apology, and his father's only reply is "Bring out the fatted calf and kill it." There are no recriminations, no moral lessons drawn or preached; the past is forgotten; there is nothing but joy: "Let us eat and celebrate because this son of mine was dead and returned to life. He is lost and is found."

If the youngster expected no such welcome, it was because he didn't know his own father, had no suspicion of the length and breadth and depth of his father's love for him. That has to be Our Savior's point, for only God could be so big. We can't begin to gauge Our Heavenly Father's love for us; let us then take the parable for what it says and believe it.

It is not difficult to sympathize with the elder son. He was the faithful one, the obedient and reliable servant. "For years now I have slaved for you and never disobeyed a single one of your commands." This was the son the father could point to and talk about with complacence.

"You have never given me so much as a kid goat to celebrate with my friends." He felt he had his rights, did the older son, and he wasn't getting them. He sees his brother's good as his own privation and becomes envious. All of which, of course, reveal the fatal flaw. In this he differed from his father. In spite of his fidelity, his conformity, his efficiency, his obedience — the love just wasn't there. Neither for his brother nor his father. His brother's joy wasn't his; his father's joy wasn't his. He wasn't big enough to make either of them another self such that their good, because theirs, should be his; their joy, because theirs, should be his. He couldn't celebrate simply because he had nothing to celebrate about.

From the father's reference to the fatted calf, it appears there was such an animal held in readiness for such an occasion, an extraordinary cause for extraordinary celebration. The aged parent explained to the elder son: If your brother's return is not such an occasion, then what is?

Were there celebrations in heaven, Our Savior would have us understand, the sinner's return would be an occasion for such. Not because heaven stands in any way to profit, but because this is the sinner's great good, and a great good, consequently, in the sight of Almighty God who loves him.

23

FIFTH SUNDAY OF LENT

LAZARUS

(Year A; John 11:1–45)

The incident from St. John that is this Sunday's Gospel selection is one of those narratives more or less rare, it would seem, in the Gospels, in which the Evangelist is concerned with recounting not merely the event itself, but also something of Our Savior's emotional response at the time. St. John, who clearly was a witness (for "Let us go also, that we may likewise die with Him," said the Apostle Thomas), can neither recall nor recount the event many years later without simultaneously recalling and recounting Our Savior's feelings so forcefully manifested on the occasion. When Jesus encountered Mary weeping and the Jews who were with her, "He was deeply moved in spirit, and troubled," says St. John, and then later at the tomb of Lazarus, "Jesus wept."

There is something somewhat disturbing about all this, in turn, to the devout Christian man as he contemplates the Gospel narrative. A sign of weakness, it would appear to be, and of a certain passivity, of a certain lack of control, perhaps, on the part of the Lord Christ. And emotional distress is, in itself, a departure from the state of habitual calm, of peace and tranquility, of order that ought to characterize rational man, and, *a fortiori*, the Incarnate Word.

If St. John took that emotional stress of Our Savior so seriously that he should recall and record it, St. Thomas in his commentary on John regards it with equal seriousness.[1] From this manifestation of feeling on the part of the Lord Christ, he would learn, and have us learn, what is right and just and reasonable in such matters.

---

[1] c. 11, lect. 5.

However deep Our Savior's agitation may have been, what is first remarkable about it is its transparent unselfishness. For His feelings arise from the sorrow of another. "When Jesus saw Mary weeping and the Jews who were with her ... " The distress of His friends leaves Him not unmoved; He is that unselfish that He makes it His own. What evil has befallen them has befallen Him.

His distress clearly springs from his *pietas*, His devotion to His friends, devotion that can characterize only the most unselfish of men. And this is a right cause, says St. Thomas, and a just one, that one should be disturbed over the sadness and evil of others, and he cites Romans: "Rejoice with those who rejoice and weep with those who weep."[2]

"*Infremuit spiritu*," writes St. John. "He was deeply moved in the spirit." Mortal man can be at fault in regard to his feelings, as we know full well. He can be carried away and his reason strangled so that he cannot think straight. Often enough his emotional response is disproportioned to the event, the effect to its cause.

St. Thomas, with his own characteristic *pietas* toward the word of God, gives serious attention to these words: "*infremuit spiritu*," Christ "was troubled in spirit." The spirit is opposed to the material, and as such, the mind to the sensitive nature. St. John is telling us something by the word "spirit." He is telling us that in Our Savior's case all was as it should be, feelings controlled by reason and will. The Lord Christ was moved to the extent that He rightly willed to be moved — nothing disordered, nothing disproportioned.

Our Savior was deeply moved, says St. John, but the Evangelist is no more specific than that. St. Thomas, however, considering the Latin "*infremuit*," judges, surprisingly but from the word itself, that the Lord Christ, as He met Mary and her friends, was actually in the throes of anger and indignation.

The occasion was the death of His friend, and He was angry that this sort of thing should occur at all, that this sort of tragedy should be necessary at all. His was the anger of a man faced with woe that did not have to be, a tragedy that could have been avoided had man obeyed, for death was inflicted as a punishment for sin.

---

[2] Rom 12:15.

It is indignation also, indignation over the cruelty of that implacable enemy of our human nature, whose malice and wiles brought this and all such tragedies into this world. It is almost as if, says St. Thomas, Our Savior on the occasion of the death of His friend was arousing His own anger at him against whom He would soon do battle and, on Calvary, vanquish forever.

Seen in a certain light, says St. Thomas, the raising of Lazarus falls into a pattern with other events in the life of the Lord Christ. Christ is true God and true man. Consequently everywhere, or almost everywhere in the single events of His life, signs of His divinity are found intermingled with signs of His genuine humanity.

Nowhere, for example, is the weakness of human nature more apparent than in the events of Holy Thursday and Good Friday, in His passion and death. Yet at the instant of His death the sun was hidden, the rocks split, and the bodies of the saints arose from their tombs. When He lay as an infant helpless and wordless in the manger, a star shone in the heavens, angels sang His praises, kings offered Him gifts. In the incident of this day's Gospel, He was about to manifest His divinity by a stupendous miracle proving Him the Lord of life. Here, too, the humanity of the Incarnate Word is evident in the Gospel narrative. It is most evident in the human feelings recorded, human feelings controlled, but deep and genuine nonetheless, evoked at the sorrow of His friends.

24

FIFTH SUNDAY OF LENT (2)

"WHOEVER LOVES HIS LIFE"

(Year B; John 12:20-33)

"Whoever loves his life will lose it," says the Lord, "while whoever hates his life in this world preserves it to life eternal." The passage is paradoxical enough, and puzzling. The theologian himself, St. Thomas, in his commentary on this part of St. John's Gospel,[1] wonders how this can be, for "*omnis homo animam suam amat.*" "*Anima*" here can be either soul or life. St. Thomas takes it as soul. It makes little difference, the one being the principle of the other, and the main point is we can't conceive of anyone hating either the one or the other.

With his usual confidence in the intelligibility of Scripture, he undertakes to understand the meaning of the words. He falls back, as he usually does when he speaks about love, on the ancient definition: *amare est velle bonum alicui.* I love someone, be it another or myself, to the extent that I will that person good. Moreover, the way I love another or myself, whether well or badly, rightly or wrongly, is determined precisely by the goods that I will to the one I love. Then on this basis and speaking generally, St. Thomas distinguishes two ways that I might love another, or myself for that matter. If the goods that I choose to will for my soul really are good for this all-important part of me, really do perfect me and make me better, then I love myself *simpliciter* — simply, really, truly, genuinely, without qualification. The virtues, for example, and such goods as grace and the Trinity indwelling in my soul. In the end, all such goods are reduced to one — *summum bonum quod est Deus* — the highest good, God. Conclusion: if I will for my soul the *bonum divinum*

---

[1] c. 12, lect. 4.

et spirituale, the divine and spiritual good, then I love my soul *simpliciter* — truly, really, without qualification.

But then there is the other way. I might love my soul not *simpliciter*, but *secundum quid* — in a way, after a fashion, in a manner of speaking, according to an analogical meaning of love. I will for my soul what I deem to be goods, but my soul is no better for the goods I will it — riches, for example, says the other T(homas) A(quinas), and honors, and pleasures, and *huiusmodi* — the goods that the world sets its heart on.

And this, he concludes, is what the Lord is saying: "He who loves his life shall lose it." Love yourself *secundum quid* — will for your soul the wrong goods — and you will lose it. "Hate it in this world" — hate it *secundum quid* — and you will save it. "What doth it profit a man if he gain the whole world and suffer the loss of his soul?"

This is the honest option in life. No man can serve two masters. We cannot love ourselves both ways.

In the parable of the rich man and Lazarus, Father Abraham himself chides Dives because the goods he set his heart on in this world turned out to be not so good after all: "In your life you had good things and Lazarus evil. Now you are tortured and he is consoled."[2] Our Savior intimated the same on the Mount when He promised, "Woe to you who laugh, for you shall weep."[3]

In Our Savior's own life, of course, He loved *simpliciter*, for He willed to all, Himself included, the truest good — God His Father, to be possessed in the eternal joys of heaven. Loving so meant hating His own life *secundum quid*. Being God, He descended from heaven and became man. But He did not stop at the top, so to speak, and take His place among the comfortable of this earth. Rather He descended all the way, to the least: "He took upon Himself the form of a slave," Paul tells the Philippians. "The birds of the air have their nests and the foxes their lairs, but the Son of Man has not whereon to lay His head." "Why do you seek to stone me?"[4] In the end He was beaten and battered, carried His cross, and was broken upon it.

This He foretold. So it must be, for "unless the grain of wheat falls into the ground and dies, it remains alone. But if it dies, it brings

---

[2]Lk 16:25.   [3]Lk 6:25.   [4]Phil 2:7; Mt 8:20; Jn 10:32.

forth much fruit." A brief parable indeed, but one that is so eloquent and so clear that it needs no comment. The Master suffered and died. He brought forth much fruit.

What holds true for the Master must needs hold true for the disciple. Authentic, persevering service of Christ is not exactly easy, nor did He ever suggest that it would be. Eternal life is not to be purchased at bargain rates. The price is determined discipline of the self-seeking that goads us all. Here, too, the grain of wheat must die, if it is to bring forth fruit.

Our Lord presses His challenge, but characteristically, promises a special reward: "If a man serves me, He must follow me; wherever I am, my servant will be there also. If anyone serves me, my Father will honor him."

HOLY WEEK

25

PALM SUNDAY

Many have marveled at the control, the calm objectivity, what might almost appear the incredible detachment of the inspired Evangelists as they narrate the passion and death of the Lord Jesus. "And they crucified Him."[1] Was ever so much horror and so much significance crammed into so few words?

But it is the meaning, and not the manner, of the passion history that we wish to recall. And we wish to recall it with reverence and gratitude and docility on this first day of another Holy Week.

No matter that this meaning of the sufferings of Christ is completely familiar. It must be remembered, and remembered, and remembered again and again — out of sheer need. There are needs that do not lessen with the passage of time.

The passion of Christ is a school. To this school Christians ever come in order to learn a lesson — many lessons, in fact. Among these is courage.

In each new Holy Week this hard lesson must be restudied and relearned. Since last Good Friday there have been in many lives new wounds, new heartache, new dismal disappointment, new tears. Last year's courage is worn thin by now. We need to read again how Christ, Our Lord, was sold out and hunted down and framed and flogged and spat upon; and how men like us then crucified Him; and how, at the end of it all, He murmured through His pain, "Father, forgive them."[2]

[1]Mk 15:24.   [2]Lk 23:34.

It takes some courage to shoulder one's burden of sorrow in this world without growing into a harsh, hostile, embittered, twisted personality. It takes still greater courage to accept without voicing a complaint. There is cause enough, God knows, for crying out against the swarming and sometimes staggering ills of life. It might indeed be argued that to challenge our destiny and loudly convict our lot of injustice might even ease a little the crushing weight upon the heart. We only note that some do thus cry out, and others, like Christ, do not.

The rarest fortitude of all is what we witness when afflicted man, through a mist of tears and with a heavy heart, offers to God a prayer of simple gratitude. It is Christian sanity and Christian virtue to thank God that God's will is truly done and God's glory mysteriously achieved in me as it was in Christ, God's only-begotten Son. It is right to welcome a share in the cross of Christ. May the passion of Christ strengthen us.

26

PALM SUNDAY (2)

(Year A; Matthew 26:14–27:66)

We have just listened to St. Matthew's account of the last hours of Our Savior's mortal life. To these hours we have attached the name "His passion." We regard them as comprising a special part of His life, however brief proportionally. We regard these hours as having a special causality, proper to themselves, in regard to our salvation. And rightly so, for within that span of less than a day, He offered the sacrifice that effectively redeemed the world, the sacrifice of His own life.

"*Cuius una stilla salvum facere totum mundum quit ab omni scelere*," writes St. Thomas in his familiar hymn to the Blessed Sacrament, *Adoro Te Devote*. "One drop" of His precious blood "would have sufficed to save the world from all sin." What we sing in the hymn is of course true. Yet God decreed and the human Christ, in conformity with that decree, willed to redeem us not by one drop of His blood, but rather by a total outpouring of that precious blood in the most excruciating agony, physical and mental, that man has ever endured.

His head was crowned with piercing thorns; no square inch of His flesh was left untorn by the Roman lash; the cross was an upright rack to which the pain of the piercing nails was added; He thirsted. These agonies were the more intense because of the exquisite sensitivity of His human body, a body formed by the direct operation of the Holy Spirit, the most perfect of all human bodies.

Before it all began, in the garden, "He began to be sad and to be afraid," as the Evangelist recounts — words that give some intimation of

the unspeakable inner anguish that crushed His Sacred Heart throughout the whole of those hours. He who Himself knew not sin, who yet
understood its malice and abhorred it as only God can understand and
abhor it, took on Himself the guilt of all sins ever committed and endured
the experience of sorrow for all. He knew His agony would be vain in
respect to a vast number of those for whom He was to die — a crushing
realization, this. He suffered the loneliness of abandonment; His closest
friends deserted Him. He suffered the intense sadness of knowing that
He Himself, who came out of love to save all men, was the occasion of
the downfall of His own people. "If I had not come, they would not have
sinned," He said.[1]

Fear is a horrible inner experience when it has us in its grip. "He
began to be afraid," recounts the Evangelist. His was the fear of a man
who is about to surrender His life — in this case the most perfect and
most valuable human life ever led — and about to surrender it only after
hours of unspeakable agony, every moment of which would be inflicted
unjustly and at the hands of contemptible men.

There was simply no way in which a human being could suffer in
which He did not suffer, and suffer most intensely, during those hours
in which He wrought our redemption. Throughout it all, He allowed
Himself no thought or consideration that might alleviate the bitterness
of His torments.

One drop of His blood would have sufficed, but Divine Wisdom
had His reasons, good and sufficient, for redeeming us as He did.

Had He won us our saving grace otherwise, there would have been
something lacking, a most precious boon that His followers do have in
the passion of Christ. "Thou shalt love the Lord, thy God," is the first and
greatest commandment.[2] Christ's agonies and their intensity, suffered of
His own free will out of love for us, attest to God's boundless love of us
in a way nothing else could ever do. "Greater love than this no man has
than that a man should lay down his life for his friends."[3] Contemplation
of that passion moves us to love God in return, and in this way, proper to
itself, promotes our redemption. The saints are the ones who have loved

[1] Jn 15:22.   [2] Mt 22:37.   [3] Jn 15:13.

God the most; one and all they have been moved to that love by devotion to the passion of Christ.

By His suffering He effectively wrought our redemption. Over and beyond, by His courage, steadfastness, patience, and humility in the midst of these agonies, insults and defamations, He provided the inspiration and example we need to make the fruits of that redemption our own. We must needs meet with difficulties and pitfalls on our way — obstacles from within, in the form of our own inertia, concupiscence, and selfishness, and cruel opposition from without, from what St. John calls the world and the devil. But "I have given you an example," He said,[4] and this He did in a special way in His passion. There never has been a great saint who was not intensely devoted to the passion of Christ. All have focused their eyes on His sufferings and therein have found the motivation to grow in holiness and persevere in their labors for the Church and souls.

From the point of view of inspiration and example alone, without the passion of Christ there never would have been in His Church the holiness that, over twenty centuries, has been its adornment. Not only did He redeem us, but such was His love that He redeemed us in that way that would be most conducive to our salvation. He went all the way, so to speak, reckoning not the cost to Himself.

Finally, by the intensity and magnitude of His agony undertaken willingly out of obedience to God and for the love of God and man, He offered to the eternal Father a sacrifice most pleasing in His sight and most acceptable to Him, more loveable in the eyes of God, indeed, than the accumulated mass of all sin is odious. The debt of satisfaction He paid was not merely adequate, but superabundant, and what He gained for us is an infinite storehouse of grace forever.

During the remainder of this week, the Church would have us turn our reverent, prayerful, and grateful attention to the passion of Our Lord and Savior. And with good reason. It is not as if we played no role in what went on in the Holy City during those holy days. We were there as the final cause, the reason why it all happened. It is right that during these days we return there once again in spirit.

---

[4] Jn 13:15.

27

HOLY THURSDAY

(1 Corinthians 11:23–26; Luke 22:15–20)

"With desire I have desired to eat this Paschal meal with you." In St. Luke's account, these words begin Our Savior's final discourse to His chosen twelve in Jerusalem, the night before He died.

In the Old Law, the Paschal meal itself was a meal hallowed, set aside, sacred in memory and tradition, celebrated by Divine prescription. But Our Lord's words make it abundantly clear that this meal was to be memorable even among Paschs. For He Himself looked forward to it with yearning, with desire, with expectation.

In His Sacred Heart lay hidden the reason for His anticipation. From all eternity the Word of God knew what He would do in the course of that meal; He knew the gift He would give in the course thereof.

"Taking the bread, He gave thanks and broke it, and gave it to them, saying: 'This is my body, which is given for you' ... And similarly the chalice, after He had supped, saying: 'This chalice is the new testament in my blood, which is poured out for you.'" Through these words He gave the gift; with longing He had looked forward to the giving thereof.

The gift He gave, the heart of man could never have conceived — Himself, Divine Holiness, to abide in the form of bread on the altar and in the tabernacles, on the tongues of those who believe in Him, to make His abode in their hearts and souls, a font of grace, of wisdom, and of strength. Food He could be for His followers, food not to be transformed, rather to transform souls into the likeness of His own.

His gift must be perpetuated. Tomorrow He would offer a bloody sacrifice pleasing to the Father. By this sacrifice He would redeem the world. That sacrifice must replace the holocausts of the Old Law; because pleasing to the Father, it must, in unbloody fashion, similarly be perpetuated. Where there is sacrifice, there must be priests. "Do this in commemoration of me." He institutes a second sacrament; His twelve become the first priests of His Church. Till the end of time, His sacrifice will be offered and re-offered; His gift will be given.

For such reasons He longed to eat this Pasch with them. Not with reluctance, but with desire, Our Savior gave the gift He gave.

The shadow of tomorrow's passion prohibits solemnity; solemn celebration of the Holy Eucharist we reserve for Corpus Christi. Yet today the Church would have us recall the Last Supper and Our Savior's efficacious words pronounced in the course thereof. "As often as you eat this bread and drink this cup, you proclaim the death of the Lord until He comes," Paul tells the Christians of Corinth in the second reading of this evening's Mass. The recollection calls for a sense of wonder that the God-man should have so loved His rational creatures that He should have given such a gift.

A gift calls for thanks, and this gift calls for sentiments of gratitude as profound as these souls of ours are capable of. It calls for a return of love to Him who has so loved us.

It is fitting that this same recollection should awaken also some measure of regret, of regret that we who have so often received the font of Holiness are not ourselves holier. In the Eucharist He comes to us; without fail He brings with Him grace; on our part we have reason to regret the spirit of routine on account of which the grace is less than it might be. We have reason to regret our hasty preparations, distracted receptions, abbreviated thanksgivings — all of which make our communions unworthy by comparison with what they might and ought to be; deny our Heavenly Guest the attention, the reverent and respectful concentration He deserves; and render ourselves the poorer in the grace that sanctifies. With humility and sincerity of heart, we offer this day's prayer over the gifts: "Lord, make us worthy to celebrate these mysteries."

28

GOOD FRIDAY

(John 12:32)

The arrival of the fifth Sunday of Lent reminds us of Passiontide soon to come. During these two weeks preceding Good Friday it is fitting, as disciples of Jesus Christ whose death was for us, to attend as occasion permits to the events that transpired from the evening of the first Holy Thursday to mid-afternoon of the following day.

If we had nothing to do with what went on during those two days, we could in all justice now disregard the memory thereof and pay these events no heed. But the fact is, in a very real sense we were there then; we played a role as the final cause of what went on there. The good of each of us was the reason why it all happened.

"And I, if I be lifted up," said the Lord Christ, "will draw all to myself." It is only right that, as occasion offers, we put ourselves there once again.

St. Thomas, in the section of the Tertia Pars devoted to the passion of Christ, investigates the kinds of pain Our Savior endured during those days of His passion.[1] Speaking of pain inflicted from without, which is the only sort Our Savior could suffer, St. Thomas wonders whether it might be rightly said that the Lord Christ endured every possible kind of such pain.

Understand "kind" in the sense of species, and the answer clearly is negative. Talk about "species" and you are introducing contraries; but contraries exclude one another from the same subject. No one could perish as did Joan of Arc, for example, and by drowning.

Father McGovern left no Good Friday sermon; this sermon for the Fifth Sunday of Lent is offered in its place.   [1]IIIa, q. 46, a. 5.

Take "kind," however, in the more generic sense, as a genus is a kind, and then it is true. That He might draw all men to Himself, Our Lord and Savior experienced in those two days every kind, and there was no kind of torment He did not suffer.

Think of the humans who tormented Him, and there is no one of the ancient world not represented. He suffered from the Gentiles — Pilate, the Roman soldiers. He suffered from the Jews, who rejected Him, condemned Him, and clamored for His crucifixion, preferring Barabbas to their Messiah. Perhaps this was His greatest pain. He came to save God's Chosen People. He became instead the occasion of their perdition. "If I had not come, they would not have sinned."[2]

He suffered from men. He suffered also from women: it was a maid, for example, who occasioned Peter's denial of Him. It was the chiefs of the people that arrested, judged, and condemned Him, but the common crowds clamored for His blood. Judas betrayed Him; Peter denied Him; His chosen twelve abandoned Him: even His closest friends contributed to His pain.

Blasphemed, He suffered in His good name. Mocked and insulted by boors and toughs, He suffered in His human dignity. Even His few possessions became a source of human grief for Him, for they were confiscated. He suffered deepest agony of spirit: sadness that crushes and, in the garden, fear of horrors to come that paralyzes.

He suffered throughout His entire body — His head from the thorns, His face from the slaps and spittle; everywhere His flesh was torn by the scourge.

He suffered through and in each of His senses: touch, from the nails, the lash, the racking of the cross; the mixture of gall and vinegar repelled His taste; He died in a malodorous place, Golgotha; the voices of blasphemers and mockers pained His ears. What He saw broke His Heart — His mother at the foot of the cross, for example, and the disciple whom He loved.

"*Cuius una stilla salvum facere totum mundum quit ab omni scelere*" is St. Thomas' thought in His hymn to the Blessed Sacrament, *Adoro Te Devote*. One drop of blood from the Incarnate God would have been enough to save the entire world from all sin. But He had to show us the enormity of sin lest we take it lightly. He had to make known to us God's boundless love; in the course of our Christian lives we would need an example of perseverance and patience, of endless courage. Such an example He provided for us. "If I be lifted up ... I will draw all to myself." That He might accomplish this end the more efficaciously, He suffered as He did.

EASTER

29

EASTER SUNDAY

(Acts 10:34, 37–43; Colossians 3:1–4; John 20:1–9)

The Gospel narrative we have just heard, consisting of nine verses from St. John's twentieth chapter, recounts a certain amount of running back and forth on the part of Mary Magdalene and two Apostles, but only one fact of importance, and this is perhaps the most momentous absence in history: the body of Christ was not where it was expected to be.

It was still dark when on the morning of the third day a handful of women stepped out of the Cenacle and made for the burial place. Within the hour a panting and tearful Magdalene burst in with her wild, senseless story. Peter and John took off at once. They returned with a simple fact: the tomb was empty.

The disciples of Christ that first Easter morning could not fathom what had happened. "They did not understand the Scripture, that Jesus had to rise from the dead." Before the day was out, the risen Lord would visit them, and they would understand: "God raised Him up on the third day and granted that He be seen … by those of us who ate and drank with Him." So St. Peter, after Pentecost, instructed the crowds in a sermon recorded in the Acts and which we read as today's first lesson.

Jesus of Nazareth had fought his enemies with determination and devastating effect, but they had prevailed. For He was dead, and death is terribly final. Never again would they have to concern themselves with "that deceiver."[1] He had died the death of the crucified, and a Roman soldier's lance had erased all doubt about the fact. But this time, for the first

[1] Mt 27:63.

95

time in history, death wasn't final at all. He was alive again. Joyous, vigorous, like one refreshed by a healthful sleep, He burst His tomb-prison and strode forth into the dawn, the victor forever triumphant over the evil alliance of Satan, sin, and death.

Our Savior's triumph makes it clear to us, first of all, that God is just and keeps His word. Through the lips of the Mother of Christ herself, He revealed that He exalts those who humble themselves for His sake. "He has put down the mighty from their seat and has exalted the lowly."[2] The Lord Christ, loving God and us, obedient to the Divine will, lowered Himself unto the lowest of the low, dying as an outcast on the cross, a worm and no man, and Him the just God has rewarded with newness of life: rich, radiant, exalted, and perfect.

As for us who are *in via*, on the way, the resurrection of Our Savior establishes us firmly in hope. We are one with Christ in His Mystical Body. He is the head, we the members. Our head is risen, alive again; we have accordingly firm reason to expect that this same condition — the happy life without shadow of stress or anxiety or pain or sorrow, the life for which we all yearn — will actually be ours. "If Christ is preached as risen from the dead, how is it that some among you say there is no resurrection of the dead?" St. Paul asks of the Corinthians,[3] and we recall the words of Job: "I know that my redeemer lives, and that I am to arise from the earth on the last day ... this hope is established in my heart."[4]

The Apostle makes it clear, too, that the resurrection of Christ should make a difference in our lives. The Christian cannot be content to be and to live as the pagans around him are and live. "As Christ has risen from the dead through the glory of the Father," he writes to the Romans, "so let us walk in newness of life," and further, "Christ who has risen from the dead does not die again ... so esteem yourselves to be dead to sin, alive to God."[5]

In those sentences we heard just a few moments ago from his letter to the Colossians, he speaks in the same vein: Christ is risen; this should make a difference, a difference in our primary concerns. Let your hearts be where Christ is: "Since you have been raised up in company with Christ, set your heart on what pertains to higher realms. Be intent

---

[2] Lk 1:52. [3] 1 Cor 15:12. [4] Job 19:25, 27. [5] Rom 6:4, 9, 11.

on things above rather than things of earth." A goal, this is, to be reached through fidelity to the sacraments and by constant and persevering prayer in our daily lives. And the Apostle ends by offering once again to his Christians of Colossae foundation for hope: "When Christ appears … then you shall appear with Him in glory." If the suffering Christ delivered us from evils, the risen Christ is the exemplar of future goods.

30

EASTER SUNDAY (2)

"The Lord Christ is risen from the dead," says St. Paul, "the first fruits of those who have fallen asleep."[1] Again, he tells the Christians of Philippi, "From heaven comes the Lord Jesus Christ, and He will transfigure these wretched bodies of ours into copies of His own immortal body."[2] The joy of Christ's followers on this Easter day is something more than just a happy enthusiasm for a stunning winner. A man brought death, and a man has brought us resurrection from the dead. Just as all have died with Adam, so with Christ all will be brought to life.

Jesus of Nazareth encountered human foes in His mortal life. He fought them with fierce determination and devastating effect, but in the end they prevailed. High priest Caiphas shrugged his shoulders and said, "It is best for us that one man should die for the people."[3] So Christ died the death of the crucified and was buried. *Et resurrexit tertia die.* On the third day He rose again. The Savior triumphed over His mortal enemies, and He never once mentions them or bothers about them again. Christ's victory is total.

What He has conquered is the evil alliance of sin and death, Satan and hell. Death He has nullified forever. He has conquered by the cleansing power of the blood He shed. It was on the evening of the Resurrection day, we recall, that Christ bestowed on His Church for all time the divine power absolutely to forgive sin. What Christ bested in His coming from the tomb is the leering reality that lurks behind evil, that implacable fallen angel who will not give over his plan to poison all that is good, that

---

[1] 1 Cor 15:20.   [2] Phil 3:20–21.   [3] Jn 11:50.

invisible malice who if he were capable of delight would delight that so many men no longer believe in him. The resurrection says "Evil can be beaten. Evil is beaten — by, in, and with Christ."

The majestic bursting of the tomb-prison on that far off Sunday morning must mean joy to the Christian, as it meant joy to Christ. The Lord Christ, stout warrior that He was, did rejoice in His victory, and His joy appears characteristically in His quiet, gentle, gracious serenity. It is impossible to listen to the risen Christ as He softly calls Magdalene by name, as He says to His scared disciples, "Peace be with you," as He asks the bumbling man who had so furiously denied Him, "Simon, son of John, dost thou love me?" — it is impossible thus to observe this most wonderful conqueror and remain a stranger to Christian joy.[4]

What remains for Christian man is only to stretch out his hand to the grace and merits of Christ, and so come to his share in the happiness that Christ has won.

[4]cf. Jn 20:16; Jn 20:19; Jn 21:16.

31

SECOND SUNDAY OF EASTER

(John 20:19–31)

That first Sunday evening, as St. John records, there occurred the reunion. The Lord Christ came "and stood in the midst of them." Our Savior kept His promise made at His Last Supper with His twelve: "I shall go and I shall come again to you."[1] He stood in their midst so that, trusting in their own eyes, all present would know that it was He.

We can almost hear the calm, gentle, gracious serenity in His voice as He greets them: "Peace be to you."

Our Savior had the happy faculty of saying the right thing at the right time; at that moment the hearts of His disciples must indeed have been far from peaceful.

They suffered guilt, for one thing — the unsettling and humiliating realization that they had been proven cowards and betrayed Him. One had emphatically denied Him; others had fled. As it had been written, "I shall strike the shepherd, and the sheep of the flock will be dispersed."[2] From this guilt He freed them; His expression, His voice, His gestures radiated forgiveness. He offered them instead the peace that comes from reconciliation with God. For this reconciliation precisely He had wrought by His passion and death.

They were grim and dispirited, and their despair was black. They had seen their incomparable leader struggle to within sight and sound of stunning victory, only to be crushed with the finality of death. But this time, for the first time in history, death was not final at all. For He stood in the midst of them, the victor over sin and death forever. Now

[1] Jn 14:3. [2] Zech 13:7.

their faith was confirmed; theirs was now the peace that comes from knowing that in believing in Him they had been right all along and could not lose.

Paralyzing fear is incompatible with inner peace. The disciples of Christ were so tense with fear of the Jews that they had locked the door of the place where they were — a forlorn gesture if any arresting party had come, as in Gethsemane, with the muscle of a platoon of Roman legionaries. This fear He dissipated. He is with them again. He has faced the worst His enemies could bring to bear and has triumphed. Now let come what may; there is nothing to be afraid of. "My peace I give you, my peace I leave you." Enduring peace among any group of men on this earth is one unmistakable sign of the presence of God.

"Peace" was frequently enough on the lips of the risen Christ. Peace was His to possess and to share, and the peace that was His is the only peace that is really worth anything. It is the peace that results from having resolved the conflict. He had side-stepped no issues; He made no truce with the forces of evil. His enemies were the enemies of God, and He fought them with fierce determination and devastating effect. He bore the toil and the labor, the opprobrium and the pain until the source of the strife had been squarely faced, struggled with, and laid to rest. Then He could say, and did, "Peace be with you."

He took a little supper then to establish His reality.[3] "Peace be with you," He repeated.

But inner peace apart from peace with God cannot be. For peace follows unity — first and foremost, unity with God. Sin is destructive of tranquility of soul because it destroys that unity. If peace is to prevail in His Church, then the divine power to free from the divisive force that is sin must similarly reside therein. He breathed on them: "Receive ye the Holy Spirit; whose sins you shall forgive, they are forgiven. Whose sins you shall retain, they are retained."

At His Last Supper, He had ordained His twelve as His first priests. Then He conferred on them the power to offer sacrifice, to consecrate the Eucharist. Now He confers on them the second power constitutive of His priesthood. As instruments of Christ, His priests have the power to

[3]Lk 24:41–42.

judge, yes or no, the power to loose from the bonds of sin and to loose efficaciously.

"I believe in the Holy Catholic Church, the forgiveness of sins … " Thus we profess in the Creed that the divine power to forgive sins resides in Christ's Church. It is fitting that Our Savior and Lord should have bestowed this power so to vanquish sin on His Resurrection day, the same on which He triumphed over death, the consequence and companion of sin.

We have need of this sacrament of reconciliation; therefore He bestowed it. In our weakness, we fall. After the saving waters of baptism, we fall again. We make our firm resolves and fail to live up to them. We need to be freed from guilt; we need to reestablish our peace and friendship with God.

We need a manner of forgiveness proportioned to our nature. Pray we to our God for forgiveness in the seclusion of our chambers, and we have no sign that such forgiveness is ever granted. But in the words of absolution from the lips of the priest, we have the assurance that rests firmly on faith.

One recalls the days not too long ago when every priest in the parish was in his box Saturday afternoons and evenings, and there were lines waiting at all the doors. This situation no longer prevails, but it was good, that. It meant, for one thing, that Catholics were more often taking time out to search their souls and ask the all-important questions: How am I doing? How goes the battle? How fares my eternal salvation?

More important, sacraments are still what they were intended to be and what they always have been: sources of grace and the indispensable means of holiness within the Church of Christ. The sacrament means grace and all that comes with it — stronger faith, firmer hope, greater love. It means deeper and closer union with God, which is holiness; and in the measure, moreover, that individual members grow in holiness, so grows the Church as a body.

The sacrament of penance is a gift which the Lord gave on Easter day to reconcile us and, in reconciling, to sanctify us, to communicate to us His peace. Let us neither fail nor hesitate to take advantage of this gift.

32

THIRD SUNDAY OF EASTER

EMMAUS

(Year A; Luke 24:13–35)

From this day's Gospel narrative taken from St. Luke, it is clear that resurrection did not change the Good Shepherd. Two of His disciples, shaken by the crushing defeat of Good Friday, defected. In the hour of need and challenge, they abandoned the company of the faithful. But Our Savior went in search of His strayed sheep. Kindly, gently, relying on their own acquaintance with the Scriptures to convince them, He brought them back.

A remarkable aspect of this appearance of the risen Christ is that on this occasion alone, among the ten or so apparitions recorded, He so appeared as not to be recognized by His own. "Their eyes were held," says St. Luke "so that they did not recognize Him." St. Mark, who makes but brief mention of the event, gives as the reason for this that Christ appeared to them "*in alia effigie,*" in some other form, as another, not quite as Himself.

St. Thomas, in the section of the Tertia Pars where he treats of the appearances of the risen Christ, investigates the reason for this: "Why, on this occasion, *in alia effigie?*"[1]

He finds the reason in the interior mental disposition of the two disciples themselves: "*Videbantur circa fidem tepescere*" — "They seemed to have grown lukewarm about the faith." Their belief in Him had weakened. "We were hoping — *sperabamus* — we used to hope — that it was He who would redeem Israel," they explained to Christ, still unrecognized.

---

[1] IIIa, q. 55, a. 4.

To the other disciples, whose faith was firm and who were willing to accept Him for what He claimed to be and was, Our Savior appeared as unmistakably Himself. But to the two in whom the light of faith had begun to grow somewhat dim, who had begun to doubt, who were less willing to accept Him at His word for what He claimed to be, He appeared in a blurred and obscure way, so to speak, not clearly recognizable as Himself. It is as if He proportioned the clarity of His appearance to the vividness of the disciples' vision of Him. As St. Gregory expresses it: "As He was in their minds, so He appeared to them."

It all seems to be an instance of a general principle: so long as one's faith remains doubtful and distant, one's perception of the truths of faith must remain always obscure and confused.

He made use of the Scriptures as they walked, to make it clear to them that this was the way it was to be with the Messiah: "He would have to undergo all this and so enter into His glory." When they saw then the fulfillment of the prophecies, they were willing to believe and did. Then He revealed Himself to them "in the breaking of the bread."

It is quite clear from the New Testament that Our Risen Savior's association with His chosen ones was remarkably different from His former companionship with them from the early days until Good Friday. For during His public life He was continually with them. But His association for the forty days after His resurrection was an intermittent presence, according to the sacred record, consisting of some ten appearances at irregular intervals, five of them on Easter day itself, some in Judea, some in Galilee.

St. Thomas, good theologian that he is, convinced that there is a reason for all Our Savior did and for the way He did it, seeks the explanation of this difference and finds the reason in the fact that, with regard to His resurrection, there were two truths that Our Savior had to make abundantly clear to His disciples.[2] The number, the manner, and the circumstances of His appearances must be such as to establish those truths.

There was the fact of His resurrection, first. But then secondly it was imperative that His followers catch some glimpse of the glory of

---

[2]IIIa, q. 55, a. 3.

Him who arose from the dead, that they understand what it means to be glorified.

For the first it sufficed that He appear to them, and to many of them, not just once but on several occasions, that He converse familiarly with them, eat and drink with them, be touched by them.

He made it clear, for instance, that what they beheld was no vision or phantasm. There is no knowing power more certain than the sense of touch. "Touch and see," He said, "that a spirit does not have flesh and bones such as you see that I have," and He enjoined Thomas to place his fingers in the wounds of His hands. He made it equally clear that this was the same Jesus of Nazareth that was crowned with thorns and scourged, carried the cross and was crucified, for He showed them the scars that remained from His wounds.

He ate a little supper, responded to those who addressed Him, and greeted those present. He conversed with the disciples and discussed the Scriptures, in all this manifesting the reality of His human life on all three levels: the vegetative, the sensitive, and the intellective.

On one occasion He instructed some of them to let down their nets for a catch, and they filled those nets almost to breaking, thus making it clear that the risen Jesus of Nazareth is, as He was, a Divine Person.[3] This same fact He established again at the end when before their eyes He ascended into heaven, but "no one ascends to heaven but He who descends from heaven, the Son of Man who is in heaven."[4]

But His second purpose was to communicate to His own that His risen life was now a glorified life, and this purpose precluded constant and continuous companionship with them, much as this might have been the preference of His Sacred Heart. "He was unwilling to associate with them continuously," says St. Thomas, "lest He should appear to have risen to such a life as He previously had."

He mentioned on one occasion, "the words which I spoke to you when I was still with you."[5] "When I was still with you" are strange words from one who at that moment was in their midst. But there was reason for His speaking so, for although He was with them, yet in another real

---

[3]Jn 21:6.   [4]Lk 24:51; Jn 3:13.   [5]Lk 24:44.

sense He was not with them. Previously, His life had been of the same sort and kind as theirs: a physical human life, yes, but a life subject to sadness and fear, and pain and death. Now His life was again, of course, physical and human, but different in sort and kind from theirs, a life on a very different plane. In a very real sense, therefore, although He was with them, He was not with them. Inappropriate then would it be if He were to be one of them as He had been before.

But in more concrete ways He gave them a glimpse of what it means for a human being to be in that state we call glorified. "Although the doors were bolted," for instance, "He stood in their midst."[6] And we read in today's Gospel selection: "Suddenly He vanished from their sight." To be seen, not to be seen — this was in His power.

In sum, it is clear from the Scriptures that the risen Christ leads the life of a person with persons, though intermittently, and it is a happy life, a life without shadow of stress or anxiety or pain or sorrow. It is that other and better life for which we ourselves so honestly and reasonably long. On Resurrection morn, Christ strode forth from the tomb alive again. By so rising, He pledges to the believer ultimate entrance into such a life: rich, radiant, exalted, and perfect. With cunning beyond all that is human, the tempter whispered to Eve: "You yourselves will be like gods."[7] He lied, but his words, ironically, were true. The risen Christ is our pledge of their truth.

---

[6]Jn 20:19.   [7]Gen 3:5.

33

FOURTH SUNDAY OF EASTER

(Year B; Acts 4:8–12; John 10:11–18)

We human creatures need images. Simply, we are not angels, but humans. Seeing, hearing, touching — these are the beginnings of all our knowledge. So even our most abstract concepts we need to link to some image of something seen or heard or felt. For this reason the Bible is, to some extent at least, a picture book. We need pictures, so Scripture pictures God for us. The images are deficient, and that Israel thoroughly grasped this truth is evident from its rooted horror of the graven image. Yet God's appointed spokesmen never hesitated to describe the Lord in terms human and vivid. There is a risk in this, as there always is in analogies. But it is a risk they chose to run. So also did Christ.

Israel was a rustic people, once nomadic. For them, sheep-raising went back to Father Abraham. Hence nothing could have been more natural to them than to describe the relationship between God and His Chosen People as that between shepherd and flock. "The Lord is my shepherd; I shall not want" reads one of the more celebrated psalms.[1] The image evidently appealed to Our Savior as just and apt. But He made the usual startling change in the use of it, the change that He can honestly make because He and the Father are one. Instead of repeating "God is your shepherd," He said simply, "I am the good shepherd."

As these words actually occur in the tenth chapter of St. John, they strike us in fact as the second part of a classic instance of mixed metaphor. Just a few verses before, the Lord Christ refers to Himself as the gate to the sheepfold; He adds that the shepherd enters through the gate.

[1]Ps 23:1.

But then He claims, "I am the good shepherd."

Actually both images are just, and Our Savior would have us learn something from each. Consider the sheepfold as representing the hidden things of God — God as He is, and God's will in our regard — and it is indeed through Christ that we enter into the sheepfold: He is indeed the gate. From His lips come the words that are the way to God. He it is that reveals God to us and what God would have us do. "I am the way and the truth," and "Who sees me, Philip, sees the Father."[2]

If He is so the gate, He is no less the shepherd. If the shepherd leads his flock hither and thither from this green patch to that, it is finally that they may find nourishment, that they may be fed. The Lord Christ then is the shepherd extraordinary, and He would seem to have earned that title primarily at the Last Supper. "This is my body … This is my blood … Do this in commemoration of me."[3] The food with which He feeds His own is His own body and blood, nourishment for the soul *par excellence* unto eternal life.

Nor is there any conflict in the two images. Combine the two — gate and shepherd — and it is simply that another truth emerges. If He is both, this means simply that He enters into the hidden things of God through Himself. And indeed He does: as the Son, the *Verbum*, He is God and beholds the hidden things of God. In manifesting God, He manifests Himself.

But we must enter through Him. "Lord to whom shall we go?" asked Peter. "You alone have the words of eternal life."[4] The truths that fall from His lips are the good seed that must find fertile ground.

If the Lord Christ shares His title of "gate" with no one, this is not so with His title of "shepherd." He appointed His own shepherds. For example, Peter He enjoined: "Feed my sheep, feed my lambs."[5] All His Apostles became in time shepherds. So, too, are all good bishops. As the prophet Jeremiah foretold, "I will give you shepherds after my own heart."[6]

"I am the good shepherd," says Our Savior, and He develops the notion. "The good shepherd lays down his life for his sheep."

Apply these words to the literal shepherd and they will not, of course, hold true. The shepherd, if he has some concern for the dumb,

[2]Jn 14:6, 9.   [3]cf. Lk 22:19–20.   [4]Jn 6:68.   [5]cf. Jn 22:15–17.   [6]Jer 3:15.

wooly cuties entrusted to his care, might indeed be expected to suffer some inconveniences for their good — but never to lay down his life for them. No number of ovine lives can be worth one human life.

But the case is quite different in regard to the metaphorical shepherds, the shepherds of souls. Our Savior's words make clear the awful responsibilities of their office and the frightening exigencies thereof. They must love their flock, first of all. Then the spiritual good of his own outweighs the individual shepherd's physical life. Endanger that good, and he must be ready to suffer any loss: the good shepherd lays down his life for his sheep.

What Our Savior seems to be here demanding of His pastors, basically, are charity and courage. These, indeed, are always in order. What courage will be demanded of His pastors in years to come, we cannot foretell. Clearly, at the moment it is courage to hold fast to Christian truth in the face of relentless corrosive opposition, opposition even from within.

The Church seems to see the Lord Christ as here indicating courage, too. For to this rare virtue she directs our attention also in other parts of the Mass. St. Peter, himself in time a good shepherd, was much in want of courage that first Holy Thursday night. But he shows it in abundance as he stands up and boldly addresses the crowds in today's first scriptural passage. And then there is the reference in the opening prayer: "Almighty God, strengthen us through the courage of Christ, Our Good Shepherd."

34

FOURTH SUNDAY OF EASTER (2)

(Year C; John 10:23–30)

The incident that occasioned these words we have just read from St. John's tenth chapter occurred in Jerusalem in the temple precincts, in the area known as Solomon's Portico. It was in the corresponding area in the original temple that Solomon had stood when, by his prayers, he dedicated that house of worship, as we read in the Third Book of Kings.

In that section of the temple grounds, says St. John, "*Judaei cirmcumdederunt eum.*" Those enemies of Christ to whom St. John habitually referred as "the Jews" stood around Him, surrounded Him, literally. The word recalls the Twenty-first Psalm: "*Tauri pingues obsederunt me.*"

As if the truth of things were their only concern, they require of Him, "How long will you torment our minds? If you are the Christ, tell us openly." It was a strange demand to make of one who had proclaimed His message always in the temple and in the synagogues, on the hillsides and where the crowds were, and who could say to Annas at the end of His life, "I have always spoken openly, and in private have taught nothing."[1]

The stubborn bad faith of those He had come to save was agony to His Sacred Heart. What more could He say to them? What more could He do to substantiate the truth of what He claimed? "I speak to you, and you do not believe me." By words alone they could not be persuaded; no more will they admit the testimony of the wonders He wrought before their eyes. "The works which I do in the name of my Father, these give testimony about me." "Every tree is known by its fruit."[2] Such works could be wrought by none other than God, and this they knew full well.

---

[1]Jn 18:20.   [2]Lk 6:44.

Therefore they had no excuse. "If I had not done these works among them, which no one else had done, they would not have sinned. But now they have seen, and they hate both me and my Father."[3]

In words plain and unmistakable, He charges them with the reason for their unbelief: "You do not believe because you are not of my sheep."

Why they are not of His flock is perhaps not so much the question. The question would rather appear to be why those who are, are, and to this, in turn, no answer can be found apart from the Divine election. "*Illi qui eliguntur ex Dei miseratione assumuntur,*" says St. Thomas in His explanation of this same passage. "Those who are chosen are chosen by the mercy of God."[4]

At any rate the demand of the *Judaei* proves the occasion of a brief instruction by Our Savior about the sheep of His flock and their shepherd, their ties with Him, and His with them.

What characterizes His own, first and foremost, is attention to Him. "*Vocem meam audiunt*" — they hear my voice. He teaches the truth; the sheep of His flock listen, understand, accept, believe. He commands, directs; the sheep of His flock accept, obey.

To the faith of His own and to their obedience, He on His side responds with fond recognition. "*Ego eas cognosco.*" "The Lord knows those who are His," says Paul to Timothy.[5] "I know them," says the Lord, but the knowledge whereof He speaks is more than just that: "I know them" with a knowledge shot through with love and approval.

The sheep of His flock listen. More than that, "*sequuntur me.*" They follow Him. They bend every effort to imitate Him, to think as He thought and acted, to love what He loves and despise what He despises, to follow the way of mildness and innocence prescribed on the Mount of Beatitudes, the way of union with God and love of fellow man taught at the Last Supper. "Christ suffered for you, leaving you an example that you may follow His footsteps," writes Peter in his first epistle.[6]

They so follow, and to their following the Good Shepherd responds, "I give them eternal life." They follow me now on this earth in this way, and I will have them follow me afterwards, entering into the joy of eternal life.

---

[3]Jn 15:24.   [4]*Commentary on the Gospel of John*, c. 10, lect. 5.   [5]2 Tim 2:19.
[6]1 Pet 2:21.

In the few phrases that remain in this brief Gospel passage, Our Savior comments on this eternity to which He has just referred. He proves, as it were, that this life is eternal. God, its source and object, is eternal. "This is eternal life: that they may know Thee, the only true God, and Jesus Christ, whom Thou hast sent."[7] "They," on their side, His own whom He rewards, "will not perish." The time for failure is past. They are beyond, moreover, the reach of him who is the enemy of our human nature, the prince of this world who goes about seeking whom he may devour: "No one shall snatch them out of my hand," as the fallen archangel snatched paradise from the hand of Adam. "For the Father is greater than all … and I and the Father are one."

So speaks the Lord Christ in the Gospel of today's Mass about His sheep — what is incumbent on them, and how He in turn responds.

In accord with these same words, we beseech God in the postcommunion prayer: "Good Shepherd, look with pleasure upon your flock, and deign to lead into eternal pastures those whom you have redeemed with the precious blood of your Son."

---

[7] Jn 17:3.

35

FIFTH SUNDAY OF EASTER

(Year C; John 13:31–35)

The words of today's Gospel Our Divine Lord spoke to His Apostles toward the close of His memorable final meal with them. Dismissed by Christ, Judas had just departed from the Last Supper to consummate his treachery. At that moment when His death had become factually inescapable, Christ proclaimed, "I shall not be with you much longer," and then proceeded with His last will and testament: "I give you a new commandment: love one another."

Actually the ancient book of Leviticus had centuries before enjoined on the Israelites: "You must love your neighbor as yourself,"[1] and Christ Himself quoted this Old Testament imperative. Nevertheless there are aspects of newness about Christ's commandment of love. For one thing, Christian love of neighbor should be marked by an unqualified universalism: no one, be he stranger or alien or enemy or distressingly "different" is excluded from that love. And then our charity must follow the most exalted model: "Just as I have loved you, you also must love one another." Lastly, this willed devotion will be the very hallmark by which the Christian is known. It is part of his identity: "By this love you have for one another, all men shall know that you are my disciples."

But from all this, as we know full well from our own experience, there arises a problem. Given that this is the Lord's command to us, and given on our part a most serious desire to adhere to it, how do we go about fulfilling such a command as this? Can we compel ourselves to

---

[1] Lev 19:18.

love everyone? Can we actually make ourselves love anyone? How can we go about it?

In this English language of ours, when our love is less intense, we use the verb "to like"; where it is more intense, we use the verb "to love," itself. No matter. If we pause to reflect on the facts of the case, we find that when we do like or love, no matter whom it may be that we like or love, this affection we feel is naturally and spontaneously aroused in us because we find that object or that person somehow, in some way, good.

Just stop to consider the myriad things you love. You love many — from a cool drink on a hot day to a work of supreme art, perhaps, because of the pleasure they give you. Other things you like because they are useful for other items — like money, which everyone loves to some extent, no matter how he may protest to the contrary. What you love, you love because of some goodness you see in it.

In regard to the persons we love, the situation is similar. We might find our fellow man good because his company is pleasant, or hers; or maybe because he or she is helpful to us in one way or another. Maybe the goodness that attracts us in another is a generosity and honesty, warmth and concern, geniality and frankness that adorn that personality. No matter what the particular reason, our love for another is the natural and inevitable response to some goodness of some kind that shines forth in him and in her and draws and attracts us.

And that is the rub; that is the source of the problem. Our neighbor is not always quite so loveable. The goodness that would arouse our affection is not always abundantly in evidence. In its stead what we sometimes encounter is selfishness and crankiness, meanness and dishonesty, and traits such as these which tend to elicit anything but love.

All this the Lord knew full well, and He took it for granted. He Himself was well-acquainted with the unloveableness that is in man; no one was more familiar with it than He; no one had more woeful experience of it than He. Yet nonetheless, He loved, loved to the extent that He gave His life for all, even for those who hated and condemned Him, mocked Him, tortured Him, and actually took the life from Him.

Knowing full well the difficulties involved, He commanded us to love just the same.

So far as obeying His command is concerned, what we can do — all that we can do — is seek the good, try to find the good, be disposed to find the good. Where good is found, to the extent that it is, love will follow.

After all, no matter what the faults and blemishes of our neighbor, there has to be some goodness there because he is made to the image of God. God Himself sees good in that person, enough so that He has created him and preserves him in being and has destined him for eternal life with Himself. Christ, Our Lord, thought that much of our neighbor that He died on the cross for him. Where God sees goodness, we must. This much goodness at least I can find: he or she tolerates me, and for that I can love him.

There is another side to all this too, which is that if I am obliged to love my neighbor, then correspondingly my Christian neighbor is obliged to love me. I might not be quite so amiable myself. Then let me at least do my part to ease my neighbor's task by striving to make myself just a little more loveable.

The Lord had His own good reason for leaving with His disciples this, His last will and testament. No matter how lofty and idealistic His command might appear, or how difficult of observance, we still must admit that families, neighborhoods, towns — the entire world, in fact — would be joyous and peaceful communities, indeed, to live in, if all men would but take this command seriously and give it a try.

The Lord Christ would have love existent among His faithful and His disciples, but He would have more than that. He would have them linked, and linked inseparably and reciprocally, by the bond of that inestimable human good that we call friendship.

Where there are friends, of course there is love — of greater or lesser degree, based on a sharing in one or more goods more or less noble in which all communicate, and in which all delight. But friendship is a love that is mutual, requited. Moreover, this common bond of affection is not hidden from the friends themselves; each is aware, if only in some unformulated way, of a place in the heart of the other. Because it is so mutual, therefore, the love of friends has something of justice about it; because so mutual, the affection is all the stronger, the way doubling strengthens.

In the blessing of such friendship, the Lord would have His own dwell. He commanded them, therefore, "Love one another."

Where God's rational creatures enjoy anything together, no matter what it may be, there is some bond of affection among them, and not all human love is of the noblest. That His eleven may know, therefore, what this love ought to be that should prevail among them, Our Savior directs their attention to Himself and His love for them.

Let them look to that love of His whom they call their Lord and Master. They will find it marked, first of all, by a gratuitousness that is overwhelming, beyond comprehension. He loves His own with a love that is utterly undeserved, unmerited. Unlike ourselves, He does not hold off, nor does He wait for indications. Unlike our own, His love is not a response to signs of favor, or kindness, or good will, or affection. "It is not as if we have first loved God," says St. John in his epistle, "but rather God has first loved us."[2] "As I have loved you, so love you one another," He says.

St. John may well have had these words of Our Lord's in mind when he wrote years later: "Let us not love in word and by tongue, but in work and in truth."[3] Love worthy of the name is efficacious: it is proved by anticipation and consideration, by taking pains and by self-sacrifice. But there is nothing more a man can do for his friend than to give himself for him, and just this, the Lord Christ did. "He loved us and gave Himself up for us," writes Paul to the Christians at Ephesus.[4] "As I have loved you" — in work, that is, and in the truth — "so love each other."

Friends are alike in many ways; they must needs be — alike in their interests, for example, in their enjoyments, in their character. Friends will good to one another, for this is to love. In the measure that that in which they are alike is itself something noble and worthy, in the measure that the goods they will to each other and in which they share are genuinely goods, so the friendship itself is good, noble, commendable.

[2] 1 Jn 4:10. [3] 1 Jn 3:18. [4] Eph 5:2.

Among Christ's believers, too, there prevails a likeness, first and foremost the likeness to Him. It is the likeness wrought by grace, the likeness of the adopted son to the natural son, and on that likeness is founded Christ's love for His own. The good He wills is the highest possible good, their union with God. "Father, keep them in Thy name … that they may be one, as we also are."[5] In this way He loves, and He instructs: "As I have loved you, so love one another." Let your love be founded on the same likeness, directed to the same good.

Love for one another, like in quality to Christ's love for us, is to be the hallmark by which Christ's disciple is to be known; it is to be part of his identity. This, not thaumaturgy, nor gift of tongues, nor prophecy, nor eloquence, nor wisdom, nor fasting, nor endurance, is to be the insignia which distinguishes the disciple of Christ. "In this will all men know that you are my disciples, that you have love for one another."

---

[5] Jn 17:11.

36

SIXTH SUNDAY OF EASTER

(Year C; John 14:19–29)

The Gospel readings during these weeks after Easter are selected from Our Savior's incomparable discourse to His chosen eleven after His Last Supper. These words we have just read from St. John's fourteenth chapter form the response to a question interposed by the Apostle Jude. "Lord, how is it," he asked, "that you will manifest yourself to us and not to the world?"

St. Thomas, in his commentary on this part of St. John's Gospel, reflects on the words of this particular question of St. Jude's.[1] He remarks that it is a characteristic of the holy and the humble that when they hear praise bestowed upon them, lofty tribute paid to them, they are amazed at this and astonished. To them, praise has the character of big news. In the genuineness and sincerity of their humility, they never suspect the existence of anything laudable in themselves. Allusion thereto catches them unawares and takes them by surprise.

It was in some such spirit of astonishment that the Apostle Jude so posed the question he did. "Lord, how is it that you will manifest yourself to us and not to the world?" What evoked the exclamation was Our Savior's prior announcement: "In a little while the world will not see me, but you will see me" — words, these, that express a preference on the part of the Word Incarnate for His own little flock over the entire world. Stunned by the revelation of such a preference, the humble Jude exclaims as he does: "Why to us, and not to the world?"

"If anyone loves me, he will keep my commandments," is the

---

[1]c. 14, lect. 6

response. On the face of it, Our Savior's words, as St. John records them, appear to ignore the question asked. Yet it is all there. About those to whom God will choose to manifest Himself, the Lord Christ says much in few words. Then in a few more, He says worlds about the manifestation itself.

Briefly He lays down the conditions. The world loves Him not; because it has no love, it keeps not His commandments. The little flock, at least in their imperfect, stumbling, inchoative way, does both. He will, accordingly, manifest Himself to His own, but not to the world.

It all makes sense. Without some love of God, clearly man just won't do the minimum to make possible any communication of God to himself. He'll take no steps at all toward God, in no way approach Him — but it is "those who approach His feet that will receive of His wisdom," says Deuteronomy.[2] He'll never raise his gaze upwards, and without this, no glimpse of the Creator of heaven and earth is possible. He'll subtract no moments from the material pursuits of the earthly existence he loves, to devote to the quest for God. The dispositions just aren't there; as the world closes God out, to the world He cannot manifest Himself.

His own have been with Him for some three years. They have heard the Sermon on the Mount and hearken to Him now. They have His commandments. If their comprehension falls short, no matter; He will send the Holy Spirit who will clarify for them all that their Lord and Master has taught. If they love Him, they will keep those commandments, for love means adherence to the one loved, commitment to the one loved, willingness and desire to accommodate oneself to the will of the one who is loved.

Briefly then the Lord Christ speaks of the manifestation itself. "My Father will love him, and we will come to him and take up our abode with him."

God's love is eternal, but the effects of that eternal love are felt in time. Consequent on that initial charity and obedience, "My Father will love him."

"We will come to him." He who fills the heavens and the earth, of course does no travelling. He comes to us insofar as we are moved toward

---

[2]Deut 33:3.

Him. He comes to the souls of those who love Him, in the measure that He is there in a new way, in a way in which He was not previously — through that gratuitous, supernatural, transforming reality we call grace.

The visitation of which Our Savior speaks is nothing on the order of a luncheon date or an overnight stay. "We will take up our abode with him." With His own, those to whom He referred as "the sheep of His flock,"[3] He will remain always. "My delight is to be with the children of men," we read in the book of Proverbs,[4] and Isaiah says, "The Lord your God will rejoice over you."[5] In those who love and obey Him, He finds joy, and with them He takes up His abode.

Clearly the Lord Christ is here promising to His followers a Divine presence in their lives. In accordance with which promise, sound Catholic theology affirms such a presence — the indwelling of the Triune God — in the believer who receives Christ's commandments and keeps them, and who thus stands in friendship with God through Christ.

Here is one of those core Christian truths which, if we give them the "real assent" that Cardinal Newman speaks of, will make a positive difference in our lives. The fact is that so long as I remain in His grace, God is strongly present in my life because He is truly present in my being. In that awareness, I think and speak and act. Union with God is a most cherished goal. Actually we need seek Him no further away than our own souls; He Himself has taken the initiative and achieved the closest union.

---

[3]cf. Jn 10.   [4]Prov 8:31.   [5]Is 62:5; cf. Zeph 3:17.

37

SIXTH SUNDAY OF EASTER (2)

(Year B; Acts 10:25–26, 34–35, 44–48; Psalm 97;
1 John 4:7–10; John 15:9–17)

Today is the sixth Sunday of Easter. If we find in that title neither light nor inspiration, we might, in view of the liturgical readings, re-christen this day "Wonder Sunday" or something of that general nature. In the psalm, for instance, the Church through the lips of David urges us to "sing to the Lord a new song." The reason? "For He has done wondrous deeds … The Lord has made His salvation known … All the ends of the earth have seen the salvation by our God."

The first reading, from the Acts, recounts a major turning point in the story of the Church's early growth. For the first time a non-Jew, a Gentile, is recorded as being admitted to the new Church. Cornelius was his name — a good man, evidently, a Roman officer in Palestine. He is the first of untold millions. Henceforward the wonders of our God are no longer the cherished and jealously guarded treasure of the Jews; they are the possession of all.

The Gospel selection is drawn, as it generally is these days from Easter to Pentecost, from Our Savior's incomparable discourse to His chosen eleven after His final repast with them. This disquisition begins in St. John's fourteenth chapter and continues through the seventeenth, and about this last discourse of Our Savior, the wisest counsel we can give is: read it, and the slower, the better.

At any rate, today's Gospel narrative consists of nine verses drawn from the fifteenth chapter. We might pause at any one of them and find expressed therein some one or another of "the wonders of our God."

A case in point is the fifteenth verse: "I now no longer call you slaves," Our Savior says to His own, "I call you friends."

We have here underscored for us, in Christ's own words, the difference between the Old Law and the New. The slave obeys from fear, and it was so in the Old Law. There was always the threat attached. In the New Law there is no such threat. The Lord Christ calls us His friends: the friend does not fear; he does the will of his friend because the friend is beloved.

Friendship implies a certain equality, for friendship is among equals. Speak of equality between God and man, and you are already speaking of the wonders of our God: there is just such an equality. It is God's work, and He accomplishes it through that transforming reality that is His grace that transfigures His rational creatures, elevating them to the level of the Divine.

What defines friends is mutual love. But "it is not you who have chosen me; I have chosen you." And St. John writes in his first epistle, "It is not as if we have first loved God, but it is God that has first loved us." St. Paul corroborates: "The love of God is poured forth in our hearts by the Holy Spirit who is given to us."[1] Our love for God is itself His gift. But then consequent on this love: "If anyone loves me, he will keep my commandments, and I will love him."[2] Our Savior promises mutual love. It is not of our making: it is another "wonder of God."

The great joy of friends is to be together. Our Savior promises an enduring togetherness. "If any man loves me, I will love him, and my Father will love him, and we will come to him and take up our abode in him."[3] Our Catholic faith affirms just such an indwelling of the Trinity in the souls of those who love God. The Hebrews of old, thinking of the ark, the pillar of fire, the cloud of smoke, boasted that no other people had their God so close to them as their God was to them.[4] We have news for them.

The friend is, as St. Augustine says, and St. Thomas, another self. Speak of a friend then and you are speaking of one to whom you may easily reveal the inner secrets you would not disclose to another. "I have called you friends," says Our Savior, and He continues: "The slave does

---

[1]Rom 5:5.   [2]cf. Jn 14:21.   [3]cf. Jn 14:21, 23.   [4]Deut 4:7.

not know what his master is about, but I have made known to you all that I have heard from my Father." To His friends He discloses the inner secrets of God — through His word to be believed by faith in this life, through the glory of the beatific vision in the next.

"Fear and love — in these two words is contained the difference between the Old Law and the New," says St. Augustine.[5] The slave obeys his master from fear. The New Law promises friendship, and among friends it is difficult even to speak of obedience. I love my friend and, consequently, his will is my will, and in doing his, I am doing my own. But God has made us His friends, and so it is. In doing God's will, the one who loves God is doing his own. He is then perfectly free — poles apart from the slave.

Grace and all it entails — love, friendship, faith, freedom — these are among the wonders of our God that we commemorate this sixth Sunday of Easter. They are also among the treasures of our Catholic faith — its own proper riches. "Sing to the Lord a new song," David urges, "for He has done wondrous deeds." Yet David had no such wondrous deeds to sing of as we have. What is sad these days is that in the churches, by and large, one hardly hears of these anymore.

[5]cf. *Summa Theologiae*, IaIIae, q. 91, a. 5.

38

ASCENSION

(Acts 1:1–11; Mark 16:15–20; Matthew 28:16–20)

As of this Thursday morning, forty days have slipped away since Easter. In accordance then with the testimony of Scripture that the risen Christ remained on earth for forty days after His resurrection, we commemorate this day His ascension into heaven, the event by which the Word Incarnate brought to an end His visible sojourn among us.

We have just heard St. Luke's account of the mystery as he narrates it in the Acts, and St. Mark's as he describes it, therewith bringing to a close his Gospel narrative. Our Savior's final injunctions to His disciples on the Mount of the Ascension were brief, as they are recorded, but momentous in their import.

Moses, Isaiah, the prophets of the Old Law generally, legislated only for the Chosen People; they taught only the Chosen People; they were deputed to represent the Most High only to the children of Israel. But, "To me is given all power in heaven and earth" were the words of Christ. His kingdom is universal. Therefore, "You will be my witnesses in Jerusalem, throughout Judea and Samaria … even to the ends of the earth."

"Go, therefore, and teach all nations." The Church of Christ is not merely to take its place beside others as one among many in a diversified society, and together with others leaven the whole. Rather, Christ's Church stands alone; it is to speak to the whole world and to speak with authority. In all nations, no matter where or when, there corresponds an obligation to listen.

"Unless a man be born again of water and the Holy Spirit," Our Savior had informed Nicodemus one night many months ago, "he shall not enter into the kingdom of heaven."[1] One sacrament is absolutely necessary for salvation, hence the injunction, "Baptize them." It is the Triune God, finally, who sanctifies the soul, and therefore, "In the name of the Father, and of the Son, and of the Holy Spirit."

What His disciples are to teach is to be no doctrine of their own, for "he who speaks of himself is a liar."[2] On novelty and originality, the Lord Christ places no premium. "One alone is your teacher, Christ."[3] Hence his final instruction: "Teach them to carry out whatsoever I have commanded you."

Much of what He had commanded them they did not understand as yet. No matter. "The Paraclete, the Holy Spirit, whom the Father will send in my name, He will teach you all things and bring all things to your mind, whatsoever I shall have said to you."[4] In the light of the Spirit who would come, they would understand all, and then they would be ready.

To teach, to baptize, to form the morals of all nations — the task He imposes on them is formidable indeed, hence His promise of eternal assistance: "I am with you all days," even in the darkest and most hopeless.

"He was lifted up," says St. Mark; and St. Luke says, "A cloud hid Him from their sight."

It was by His own power He was lifted up, says St. Thomas in his explanation of the ascension.[5] By His power as God, certainly, but by His power as man, too — just as certainly, not by any power flowing from the principles constituting human nature as we know it, for upward motion is not proper to a human body. But in the ascension of Christ we catch a glimpse of what it is for a human being to be glorified. The glorified body obeys the soul, and such is its obedience that, as St. Augustine puts it, "Where the spirit soars, there will the body be." "But it is fitting," says St. Thomas, "that an immortal and glorified body would be in a glorified place, and therefore from the power of the soul willing it, the body of Christ ascended into heaven."

---

[1]Jn 3:5.   [2]cf. Jn 7:18.   [3]Mt 23:10.   [4]Jn 14:26.   [5]*Summa Theologiae*, IIIa, q. 57, a. 3.

This we profess in our Creed. "He ascended into heaven and sits at the right hand of God, the Father Almighty." Through His ascension, the Second Person of the Trinity becomes enthroned as He is, that is, in His humanity as well as His divinity. In Christ, this coarse human nature of ours has been unthinkably glorified.

In Him we have a powerful friend at court. The epistle to the Hebrews deals with this exalted truth of Christ the eternal mediator. "For Jesus is not entered into the Holies made with hands ... but into heaven itself, that He may appear now in the presence of God for us."[6] He is glorified, but nonetheless His ascension is for us. Christ is the loving Son commending to a willing Father the welfare of His needy brothers in humanity.

In the prayer of the Mass, we ask of God that we may, in a diminished way, imitate the Lord Christ in His ascension. For we beg that our minds at least may be with Him; we pray that they may habitually dwell on heavenly things.

[6]Heb 9:24.

39

SUNDAY AFTER ASCENSION

(Acts 1:1–11)

A s of this past Thursday, forty days have slipped away since Easter. On that day, in accordance with the testimony of the Scriptures that the risen Christ remained on earth for forty days after His resurrection, we commemorated His ascension into heaven, the event at which the angels marveled and by which the Word Incarnate brought to an end His sojourn among us.

The Acts describe the scene: "As they looked on, He was raised up, and a cloud received Him out of their sight."

It is fitting and right, says St. Thomas in the Tertia Pars, that the risen Christ ascended into heaven.[1] For there ought to be a certain proportion between a being and the place where that being resides. This material, changing world of ours is suitable for the likes of ourselves that come to be and pass away, that can be altered and are altered variously, in some ways for better and in others for worse. This same world is scarcely the proper residence for the Lord Christ who rose to another and better life without shadow of stress or anxiety, of difficulty or fatigue, of pain or sorrow — no longer one in quality with the residents of earth. The heavens, the place of the unchanging and eternal God, this is now the rather fitting residence for a body transfigured as was the body of Our Savior in His resurrection, transformed into a citizen of another and better city.

It is not surprising that the thought of Our Savior's ascension moves us less than does His passion and death, for example, or His

---

[1] IIIa, q. 57, a. 1.

resurrection. The connection between what He did and our own eternal good, for instance, is not quite so evident. "He died for us" is readily understandable, for His death was a sacrifice; "He ascended for us" — this is not so clear.

Yet this is the simple truth and fact of the matter. Christ's ascension is a cause of our salvation, writes St. Thomas in the Tertia Pars — not in the same way that His passion was, but a cause nonetheless, and that in more ways than one.

St. Thomas remarks, for example, that Our Savior's departure from this world of what is seen and felt and heard is more beneficial to us — *utilis* — than would have been His continued visible existence among the children of men.

For one thing, we need to take Our Savior seriously, and the Apostle Paul, when they say faith is meritorious and necessary for salvation: "Without faith it is impossible to please God."[2] But the departure of the Lord Christ offers us an occasion for faith not given to the Apostles when He walked among them day by day, and spoke and ate with them. Now even the existence of the risen Christ is an object of faith, and "Blessed are they who have not seen and have believed," says the Lord to Thomas.[3] And St. Augustine writes, "Comparison with the faithful is the condemnation of unbelievers."

Hope is a most blessed virtue without which Christian man cannot persevere. Christ has ascended into heaven and has raised up our hope. "If I go and prepare a place for you, I will come again and will take you to myself, that where I am, so also you may be."[4] In Christ and through Him, this human nature which is ours and His has found a place in heaven and there resides, giving us human individuals hope of arriving at the same blessed destination. "He ascended, opening the way before them," foretold the prophet Micah.[5]

Then there is the matter of charity, love. Love we Christ, and the affections of our hearts must needs be directed heavenwards because Christ is there. "Seek those things which are above," writes Paul to the Christians of Colossae, "where Christ is seated at the right hand of the Father."[6] "Where your treasure is, there is your heart," says the Lord.[7]

[2]Heb 11:6.   [3]Jn 20:29.   [4]Jn 14:3.   [5]Mic 2:13.   [6]Col 3:1.   [7]Mt 6:21.

In this world of the New Dispensation, this love whereof we speak is not of our own doing. It is the work of the Holy Spirit and hence a direct result of Christ's ascension. "It is necessary for you that I go," He explained to the eleven. "If I do not go, the Paraclete will not come to you. But if I do go, I shall send Him to you."[8]

Then, on His side, what He did in ascending into heaven is itself, and of itself, calculated to bring us closer to the eternal goal of our one and only earthly existence. His words must be taken seriously: "I go to prepare a place for you."[9] He is the head of the Mystical Body, and it is necessary that where the head is, there also the members should follow. As we pray in the preface of this Ascension: "that we, His members, may have confidence that we will follow where He, our head and principle, has preceded."

Christ ascended into heaven. Therefore we have a powerful mediator in court. The human Christ "entered heaven to intercede for us," says the author of Hebrews,[10] as in the Old Law the high priest entered the Holy of Holies to intercede for the people. The mere fact that Christ is in heaven in, and with, His human nature is itself an intercession for us. It is as if the Father, beholding the nature which He has so unthinkably exalted in Christ, must needs have mercy on those for whom Christ assumed that nature, and who are now His brothers in the flesh.

When He prayed for Himself in the High Priestly prayer at the Last Supper, the Lord Christ asked: "Father, the hour has come … Now, Father, it is time for You to glorify me."[11] The plea is humble and reverent, but it breathes certainty. From the whole context, from all that preceded in the life of Christ, from everything that followed, we know He was asking for no personal kudos, except insofar as His glory will be the glory both of His Father and His followers. That prayer for glory was heard: it was heard in the resurrection and ascension of Christ. We have reason to rejoice with Our Savior in His triumph; we have reason to exult also in the good that this triumph has accomplished for us.

---

[8]Jn 16:7.   [9]Jn 14:3.   [10]Heb 9:24.   [11]Jn 17:1,5.

40

PENTECOST SUNDAY

(Acts 2:1–11; 1 Corinthians 12:3–7, 12–13;
John 15:26–27, 16:12–15)

The three readings of today's Mass combine, and in combining they convey to us who read and listen an impression of an event unthinkably wondrous. We read in the passage from the Acts about the first Pentecost, on which audible and visible prodigies of a physical nature both accompanied and signified a still more stupendous, but promised, wonder of the invisible and supernatural order.

We read first of timid disciples huddled together in a house somewhere in Jerusalem at the time of the Jewish Pentecost. Then we read of a wind, loud and powerful enough to attract attention, heard and felt evidently even within the shuttered and bolted house. We read of a fire suddenly appearing and being there in the house, just as suddenly dividing itself into something in the way of tongues, each one coming to rest on the head of an Apostle.

These were the signs visible that accompanied the supernatural and invisible reality. "If I go," Christ had promised, "I will send to you another Paraclete."[1] On this day that promise was fulfilled. The promised Spirit had come.

Today with gratitude we recall that day and celebrate its remembrance. Today we turn our prayerful attention to the Holy Spirit who came, and who to this day dwells in the Church and its members.

In this school we begin each class with a prayer to this same Third Person of the Trinity. "Come, Holy Spirit, fill the hearts of Thy faithful."

[1] Jn 16:7.

Faith is a gift. The faithful are those who believe. We believe precisely because God, in bestowing the Spirit on us, has given us the grace to believe.

Humbly we acknowledge our dependence on this Spirit. Such are our attachments to this world's goods that we see and touch and enjoy, that without His help we cannot begin to love God as we ought. "Kindle in us the fire of Thy love."

From our experience we know how painfully difficult truth is to come by. Attaining it is like threading one's way through a labyrinth. Error for the most part has a grain of truth in it; it has the appearance of truth. It allures and can awaken the assent it does not deserve. This danger we humbly acknowledge. We admit our own native affinity for darkness and acknowledge our utter dependence on light from above: "O God, who by the light of the Holy Spirit didst instruct the hearts of Thy faithful." Christ the Lord had predicted: "I will send you another Paraclete, the Spirit of truth, and He will teach you all things."[2]

We have Christ's assurance that since the first Pentecost Sunday this Holy Spirit, whom He had promised, is and will be with us always. The promise is forever. The Spirit abides with the magisterium of the Church.

One time in the course of His life, Our Savior posed the question, "When the Son of Man comes, will He find faith on the earth?"[3] Actually, Divine Wisdom knew the answer to His own query, and He knew it full well. Affirmative. To His Church He gave a divine guarantee of survival: "Behold, I am with you all days,"[4] and "The gates of hell shall not prevail against it."[5] He never promised that the Bark of Peter would have invariably smooth sailing. On the contrary. But implicit in His guarantee is that the good ship would, under the perpetual and enduring guidance of the Spirit, weather the roughest seas, and would even survive an occasional mutiny.

The Holy Spirit abides always with the magisterium of the Church. Through that wonder we call sanctifying grace, He abides with and in its individual members. He could not be closer to us. He is always available to assist. We do well in this school to begin class as we do.

---

[2]cf. Jn 14:16, 26.   [3]Lk 18:8.   [4]Mt 28:20.   [5]Mt 16:18.

41

PENTECOST SUNDAY (2)

(John 20:19–23)

The Holy Spirit is mentioned, and in significant contexts too, in all four Gospels. Yet it is St. John who most decisively delineates the Holy Spirit as a Person, and who most clearly describes His functions. According to John, who is quoting Our Savior, the functions of the Spirit are three.

At the Last Supper, Christ promises to send the Spirit. He gives this Person the name Paraclete. In everyday Greek, this word meant a person "called to the side" — *ad vocatus* — of one in need of assistance. Particularly, the word has reference to legal matters: a paraclete is one called to the side of one in need in legal matters. And Our Savior does say that the Paraclete will both defend and prosecute. This mighty Advocate, acting in Christ's name and place, will steady the disciples when the storm of persecution breaks, will be their unfailing defender against a hostile and accusing world.

But also when He comes, the Paraclete will show the world how wrong it was about sin, and about who was in the right, and about judgment. The faithless, invidious world, says Our Savior, will thus be shown totally wrong, will be convicted as guilty of evil — all under the indictment of the Divine Advocate. This is true, too. In the light of the Spirit, the world is constantly being proved wrong; its solutions just don't work.

The Lord Christ continues, "The Advocate, the Holy Spirit, whom the Father will send in my name, He will teach you everything and remind you of all I have said to you."[1] Thus the Promised One will be not

---

[1] Jn 14:26.

only attorney, but teacher. He qualifies as the perfect teacher because He is the Spirit of Truth. His teaching will be of nothing new but strictly and totally confirmatory of the teaching of Christ. The Paraclete "will remind you of all I have said to you ... He will not be speaking as from Himself, but will only say what He has learned ... All He tells you will be taken from what is mine."[2]

There is, finally, the passage from St. John that makes today's last liturgical reading. With solemnity John describes what he manifestly regards as a capital event of the first Easter Sunday. Jesus breathed on them and said, "Receive the Holy Spirit. For those whose sins you shall forgive, they are forgiven; for those whose sins you shall retain, they are retained." The boundless mercy of God toward the repentant sinner is celebrated in the Old Testament, it is practiced and preached by Christ, and now it is, so to speak, built into the Church by the Spirit. Again we have an instance of community and conformity of action by Father, Son, and Spirit. The action is consoling beyond words, the divine act of forgiveness.

On this latest Pentecost we welcome anew, and with gratitude, our Advocate, our Spirit of Truth, our merciful, forgiving God.

[2]Jn 14:26; 16:13–14.

42

TRINITY SUNDAY

"**H**ow incomprehensible are the judgments of the Lord," says St. Paul in his epistle to the Romans, "and how unfathomable His ways."[1]

What the Apostle here says is so true. We marvel at man's scientific progress of the last 100 years. Yet in spite of this, the world around us, which God has made, remains ultimately shrouded in mystery. The unimaginable distances between the galaxies and the stars, and the order among them, are a marvel. The energy locked in the nucleus of an atom is a mystery, for no one understands precisely why it is there. Our own eyes with which we see, indeed these are a wonder and mystery. Biologists can describe this eye of ours: how the retina is composed of over 120 million special nerve ends called rods and over 6 million of another type called cones. They know that all these are affected by light rays. But just how and why all these intricate and tiny parts are brought into proper functional alignment in the first place, and still more so just how this so familiar but nonetheless marvelous operation we call seeing results from this stimulation, is still as much a mystery as it always was. And so it is in all of this natural world. The ultimate "why" God's creatures work as they do remains still a wonder and a mystery.

And this is only to be expected, since the intelligence is infinite of the One who planned and created, sustains and directs all this. But the intelligence of man who dedicates himself to the study of all these works is far from that.

[1]Rom 11:33.

There is wonder and mystery in the mere fact that anything exists at all. Why did God create us, and the world made for us to live in? He is infinitely good, infinitely perfect, infinitely happy. He had nothing to gain by creating other things; there is nothing in it for Him. He has no need for any element or compound, plant or animal, man or angel. His creation of all the things that are is a gift of existence — a sheer gift, an act of utter and perfect benevolence, an act of complete giving with no self-interest whatever involved. This is a generosity and benevolence such as no one of us is capable of.

Why God should be so moved by His love to give being to other things is mysterious. Why He should have made us, rather than others that might have been, is still more mysterious. Mysterious, too, are the ways of His providence. So often we cannot understand how a good God, who wants only to give of His goodness, should allow things to happen as they do. What is so difficult to hang on to, but so necessary to hang on to, is that He allows it because He loves us, and there is some good beyond it. Again the situation remains the same — the finite mind struggling to fathom the infinite. Mystery there must always be in God's works.

Today we celebrate the greatest mystery of all: the Trinity. Today is the one day in the entire cycle of the liturgical year when the Church would have us turn our minds and hearts, our grateful and adoring attention, to the mystery of God Himself — God who has created us and sustains us in being, who has made us only that we may share with Him His own eternal bliss, whom we have offended, and who has wrought our redemption — God, in sum, to whom we owe all we have and all we are.

This day, moreover, is dedicated to acknowledging God and honoring Him as He has revealed Himself to be, one God in three Divine Persons, as we pray in the preface of the Mass: "It is right that we give you thanks always, Holy Lord, Almighty Father, eternal God, who with your only-begotten Son and the Holy Spirit are one God, one Lord, not in the singularity of one person, but in the Trinity of one substance."

Clearly enough, it is idle to talk of understanding such a genuine supernatural mystery. The fact of the mystery is revealed to us. At the cost of much laborious effort and a headache or two, we are able to show that the mysterious truth cannot be proved a flat and flagrant contradiction. Moreover, with the help of the great Doctors we can push our understanding considerably beyond that. But there is a point beyond which we cannot intellectually go. Supernaturally, however, strengthened and aided by God's enlightening grace, we can perform the remarkable internal act of believing what we little understand. Such a bold step is not at all a debasing surrender, but a noble triumph.

The mystery of the Blessed Trinity is a strict supernatural mystery. What God has revealed to us is that there are three Divine Persons personally distinct from one another, but that when the Divine Father and the Divine Son and the Divine Holy Spirit are taken together, the result is one Divine Being. Faced with this solid but completely baffling mystery, the mind of man unaided by grace reels dizzily and turns away in disbelief.

But in the case of a person illumined and steeled by God's good grace, the will applies the brake to the human intellect and bids it reconsider the proposition of three Persons in one God, in the light of supernatural faith. The fact is, nature and person differ in concept, and numerical plurality of persons need not necessarily involve plurality of natures. Ultimately, however, the reality of the Trinity lies beyond the comprehension of the human intellect operating under mortal conditions. The answer is not known, nor will it be known this side of heaven's very special clarity.

What remains is for the follower of Christ to bow his head and humbly, gratefully, make his profession of faith. "I believe in one God, the Father Almighty, and in Jesus Christ, His only Son … I believe in the Holy Spirit."

As often as man reflects on this or any other supernatural mystery, so often he ends by being simply grateful for the faith that is in him. Many there are who cannot accept a God in whom there are three distinct persons, or a Christ who returned from the tomb, or a Virgin Mary whose immaculate body never suffered the corruption of the grave. Their reason for doubting is their inability to understand such deep mysteries. We do not understand either. But we know these mysteries exist, and so we believe them, and thanks be to God for that.

In the Collect prayer of this day's Mass, we acknowledge that it is to Almighty God and to no endeavors, intellectual or otherwise, of our own or another, that we owe the grace of the true faith without which the Triune God must remain for us ever unknown, ever unadored. It is an old prayer in the Church, this Trinity Sunday Collect. Mainly it is a prayer for steadfastness in our faith. Mindful that this faith is a gift of God and that such graces, once given, are not lost apart from some fault on the part of the receiver, we beg of the Triune God that we may remain steadfast in that faith and so be safe, as then we shall be, from all dangers.

43

TRINITY SUNDAY (2)

"Ibelieve in one God, the Father Almighty ... and in one Lord Jesus Christ ... and in the Holy Spirit." These words are taken from the Creed as said in the Mass.

Today is Trinity Sunday. It is a most appropriate day for some little reflection on the Creed, the declaration or ancient symbol of faith whose precise origins are veiled in the mists of time. To state the situation crudely, but not untruly: without the Trinity there would be no Creed.

To believe, or not to believe — what a tremendous difference this makes in a person's life is obvious enough. The symbol of faith which we recite in the Mass — and which, incidentally, brings to a close the first distinct part of the ritual — is a summary of what we believe. Like every summary, or formula, it is incomplete. The Catholic must, and does, believe in truths which are not mentioned here. There is the Assumption of the Blessed Mother of God, for example, and so much else that is in the catechism.

Yet a formula such as the Creed is a useful sort of thing. It reminds us regularly and conveniently of those basic tenets which, because we believe them, accept them, and hold them to be true, set us apart as Catholics. It could well serve, much more than it does serve for most of us, as a reliable handbook for that sane and commendable reflection which we term meditation.

The Creed, despite its evident Trinitarian form, may be regarded as falling into four sections, or groups of articles. The general subject of belief is, in this order, God the Father; Christ, the Word Incarnate; the Holy Spirit; and the Church. We believe in the Church: that is, within the Church of Christ we profess faith in the Triune God.

In the opening section of the Creed we proclaim our belief in the existence, the Fatherhood, and the uniqueness of God. We hold that this one God is the Creator and origin of all things. In those few phrases we really proclaim so much and such fundamental doctrine. There are no wasted words in the Creed. This is one reason why it merits at least an occasional close examination.

There follows an admirable summary of our belief in Christ, the Second Person. In a striking way we insist on His divinity — the only-begotten Son of God, true God of true God, consubstantial with the Father — before we meet any mention of His Incarnation. We gratefully genuflect as we recall His blessed assumption of our human flesh. Of course it is here that His Blessed Mother is forever enshrined in the symbol of faith. Next we bring to mind Our Savior's death as a sacrifice for us, His triumphant resurrection, His ascension, His solemn eternal enthronement at the side of His Father's majesty. Finally, we state our conviction that this same Christ will someday return as supreme and absolute judge of all mankind.

Part Three declares the existence, the procession (from Father and Son), and the equal divinity of the Holy Spirit, who with the Father and the Son is no less adored and glorified.

The closing section of the Creed contains four articles. These things we hold. There is one true Church. There is valid baptism. We believe in final resurrection and in immortality.

It would be desirable, naturally, if each of us, at every Mass in which the Creed is said, could be thoughtfully attentive to each article of the formula. But we have to be reasonable. Let's not torture this poor stumbling human intellect even under the excuse of religion. As we read the Creed on various occasions, our attention will be drawn more strongly to this point or that. Very good. But let us above all be consistently grateful for the Creed, not simply in the sense of being glad that we have the formula readily on hand, but in the larger sense of rejoicing in the gift of faith, being glad beyond measure that we find it within our power and capacity to recite the Creed honestly — believing every word of it. This is a gift, this faith, a precious gift without which we could not assent to a single sentence.

Perhaps it is part of God's gift of faith to us that we do not actually see, as we recite the Creed, what a staggering act of belief is demanded of us. "I believe" is a very big and brave and beautiful word.

II

FEASTS AND OCCASIONS

SOLEMNITIES OF THE LORD

44

CORPUS CHRISTI

It is fitting that there be in the Church a solemnity of the Eucharist, a day set aside for us who bear Christ's name to turn our attention to the Holy Eucharist, to deepen our appreciation of the inestimable boon that Christ has given us; it is fitting that there be a day to provide both the occasion and the incentive to express the gratitude of our hearts, to celebrate with deep joy this treasure that is ours from the boundless love of His Sacred Heart.

Holy Thursday suggests itself as the apt day. But over Holy Thursday hangs the shadow of the passion, and liturgical sorrow. Accordingly, Pope Urban in the year 1264 appointed the Thursday after Trinity Sunday as the solemn feast of the Blessed Sacrament that we have come in this country to call Corpus Christi. Happily, the Pope commissioned Thomas Aquinas to compose the Divine Office of the day, a commission that has enriched the Church's liturgical treasury with the sermon in the first nocturn, such antiphons as *O Sacrum Convivium* and *O Quam Suavis*, and the hymns *Lauda Sion, Pange Lingua,* and *Verbum Supernum.*

In recent years, probably for the reason that so many parishes postponed the celebration of Corpus Christi until the following Sunday for the devotion of the parishioners, the feast itself has been moved to Sunday, today.

From our earliest days with the catechism, we have known that there are seven sacraments. What distinguishes these essentially from the ceremonies of the Old Law is that as instruments of the Lord High

God they actually cause and increase in the soul of man that transforming, divinizing reality we call grace, and all that grace entails. Each one, too, has its own special fruit, the particular grace that it signifies, necessary for one part or another of the Christian life.

Through each and every one of the sacraments, the Lord Christ makes His passion efficacious, adorning the soul with the grace He earned through His sufferings and death.

Yet of the seven, there is only one that enjoys in the calendar of the Church a feast day of its own. In a very real sense, each and every sacrament is blessed. Yet we reserve the epithet for only one — the Blessed Sacrament. All are holy, for through all the Holy God makes holy the soul of man. But the Eucharist is holy in a way in which the pouring of water is not, nor the anointing with oil. Among the sacraments, the Eucharist alone is substantially holy, containing under the appearances of bread and wine He in whom dwells the fullness of grace, Christ, Our Lord, body and blood, soul and divinity. He who works through the other sacraments is Himself present in this; and this rests firmly on faith.

The Eucharist then, although not the most necessary of the sacraments, is nonetheless pre-eminent among them. If all call for reverence in their presence, this, then, for reverence the greatest and most profound.

"What can be more precious than this banquet," asks St. Thomas in his sermon, "in which there is offered to be consumed not the flesh of calves and of goats, as of old in the days of the law, but Christ, true God?"[1]

And if the Eucharist is so blessed in itself, so too is this holiest of sacraments blessed in its fruits. "Who eats of my flesh and drinks my blood remains in me, and I in him" is Christ's promise.[2] Where Christ so remains, sinfulness that is the effect of sin, proneness to sin, by His power diminishes; the Eucharist is the food of virtue, and through its nourishing influence virtue grows. By it the soul is enriched by an abundance of all spiritual favors.

We none of us are what we ought to be; but that we are not worse is owing finally to the Eucharist. We shall find in eternity that the Eucharistic Christ has wrought wonders in us. But He could do more,

---

[1] *Opusculum 57, In Festo Corporis Christi*; cf. *Office of Readings according to the Roman Rite*, Corpus Christi, Second Reading.   [2] Jn 6:56.

and would, if we rose more often to the occasion and accorded Him consistently, in accord with our faith, the devotion and loving attention that such a guest deserves.

His sacramental coming in the Eucharist merits attentive preparation; it merits some moments after Mass of loving thanksgiving, with the assistance of a good prayer book if that should help. It is in fact such a deep reverence and respect as this that we beg for in the prayer of the Mass when we ask of the Almighty "that we may so reverence the mysteries of your body and blood that we may always experience in ourselves the fruit of your redemption."

45

SUNDAY AFTER CORPUS CHRISTI

(Luke 14:16–24; Luke 22:15–20)

When Christ, Our Lord, sat down with His Apostles at the Last Supper, His first words to them were: "With longing have I longed to eat this Pasch with you." Our Lord had been looking forward to this meal for some reason known to Himself. Something momentous was going to happen. The Apostles wondered: Why this longing on the part of Christ? What was it that was going to take place? No matter what they thought, they could never have imagined the riches of the gift that Christ, Our Lord, was about to leave to them and His Church on this night before He died.

They had not long to wait for the answer. The solemn moment arrived. Our Lord took bread into His hands. He said: "Take you and eat, for this is my body." Then the wine: "All of you drink of this, for this is my blood." But it was not to His Apostles alone that He has given His flesh to eat and His blood to drink, for He added: "Do this in commemoration of me." The power to change bread and wine into His body and blood was theirs to be passed on to their successors, and the great gift was given — the gift of Himself, the source of all grace, to be the food of the souls of men for all time.

This past Thursday was the feast of Corpus Christi, the day the Church consecrates to the honor of Christ, Our Lord, present among us under the form of bread and wine. Today is the Sunday after Corpus Christi. In the Gospel of the Mass, the Church calls to our attention a parable of Our Lord's which has an application to the gift of the Holy Eucharist.

A certain ruler prepared a banquet; he invited particular people to be his guests at that banquet. He extended the invitations to the free meal: how he wanted them to take advantage of his invitation. None of them did. They made excuses and stayed away.

When Our Lord said, "This is my body," and "Do this in commemoration of me," He too, like the ruler in the parable, prepared a great banquet. He extends to all the members of His Church the invitation to partake of that banquet. He wants you to partake of it for your own good. He Himself has nothing to gain by giving us His flesh as food for our souls; you are not doing Him a favor when you receive Him in Holy Communion — you are only allowing Him to do good for you. He has left this gift for the good of the Church; He wants its members to take advantage of this gift. To obey the laws of God and the Church day after day and year after year and so save our souls is extremely difficult. By our own strength alone, we cannot do it: "Without me you can do nothing."[1] But He has not left us to ourselves. He has given us Himself as the source of grace and strength for our souls; that is the purpose of the Holy Eucharist and what it accomplishes. "I am the living bread which has come down from heaven. If any man eats of this bread, he shall live forever; and the bread which I will give is my flesh for the life of the world."[2]

In spite of the greatness of the gift, in spite of its necessity for our eternal salvation, there are those who make excuses and do not take advantage of it. They put it off — not this week because they have this to do, not the next because they have something else to do. And the soul, deprived of its food, grows weak and starves. The ruler in the parable said that none of the excuses were acceptable: "I say to you, none of those that were invited will partake of my banquet." Our Lord said the same about the Holy Eucharist: "Unless you eat of the flesh of the Son of Man … you shall not have life in you. He that eateth my flesh and drinketh my blood hath everlasting life, and I will raise him up on the last day."[3]

---

[1] Jn 15:5.   [2] Jn 6:51.   [3] Jn 6:53–54.

He has given the gift. He is there, present in the Blessed Sacrament, ready and anxious to come into your souls with the grace you need to lead a Catholic life and save your souls. It is up to you not to make excuses, but to take advantage of that gift.

46

CHRIST THE KING

(1 Corinthians 15:20–26, 28; John 18:33–37)

Today the white vestments have appeared, displacing the familiar green which is the color of this liturgical season. The appearance of the white on Sunday betokens something special about this day: it is a day, liturgically speaking, above the ordinary, a solemn and exalted feast day. And such indeed is the case, for we venerate this day Our Lord and Savior under the title of Christ, the King.

It is a relative newcomer, this feast, to the calendar of the Church. "Acceding," in his own words, "to the prayers of many cardinals and bishops and faithful," Pope Pius XI instituted this liturgical feast through the encyclical *Quas Primas* in 1925, a Holy Year. His Holiness appointed the last Sunday in October for the celebration, and so it remained until the recent wave of change swept it into its present situation — the last Sunday in the liturgical year.

If this feast is thus rather new in the Church, the truth commemorated thereby is not. The references are there, for instance, in the liturgy of the Mass, as we have heard in these last few moments. "Christ must reign," writes St. Paul, "until God has put all enemies under His feet." And Christ Himself, according to His celebrated preview of the last judgment that is this day's Gospel selection, tells us that He "will sit upon His royal throne, and the King will say to those on His right, come, you blessed of my Father."

The psalms, the prophets, the New Testament abound with references to the kingship of the Messiah: "I have established my kingdom upon Zion, my holy mountain," and "The Lord said to me: Thou art my son; this day have I begotten thee. Ask of me and I will give thee the Gentiles for thy inheritance and the ends of the earth for thy possessions." The prophet Malachi foretold: "'From the rising of the sun until its setting, great is my name among the Gentiles; and in every place there is offered to my name a clean oblation because my name is great among the Gentiles,' says the God of hosts."[1]

St. John in his eighteenth chapter recounts Pilate's interrogation of Jesus of Nazareth on the subject of His kingship. We can almost hear the incredulous astonishment and the sarcasm and ridicule in Pilate's voice as he puts his first question: "You, are you the king of the Jews?"

In Our Savior's reply, the affirmative answer is implicit: "My kingdom is not of this world." "My kingdom" — I do indeed possess a kingdom. There is no denial on Christ's lips that His kingdom is in this world, for it is indeed, its citizenship composed in part of men on the way to eternity. But His kingdom is not of this world: the ends for which He has established it are outside of and above and beyond the ends for which the world's kingdoms are constituted; it transcends both the aspirations and the territorial bounds of this world's kingdoms; its common good is not passing and transient, but eternal — God Himself, to be enjoyed without end. So too are the means to its ends essentially of another sort: "If my kingdom were of this world, my ministers would strive that I should not be delivered to the Jews."

"My kingdom is not of this world." On these words of Christ, St. Augustine has a comment or two to make:

> "What a stupendous thing it was for the King of the ages to become King of men. For Christ did not become King of Israel to exact tribute, to equip armies with swords, nor subject visible foes. He became King of Israel that He might rule over men's souls, counsel them about eternity that He might lead to the kingdom of God those who would believe in Him, hope in Him, and love Him. Accordingly, it was not to increase His power — it was condescension on His part that made Him, the Son of God

---

[1] cf. Ps 2:6, 7–8; Mal 1:11

co-equal with the Father, the Word by whom all things were made, wish to become King of Israel. It was an indication of His mercy: it did not augment His power.[2]

"Art thou then a king?" Pilate asked. "Thou sayest that I am a king." Our Savior so framed His reply that He does not openly profess to be a king, for He was not, nor is, according to Pilate's understanding of the word "king." Yet He does not deny His kingship, for He is the King of kings.

The king, by definition, is opposed to the tyrant, and the difference is that the former rules for the common good. His it is to legislate, to judge according to his laws, to enforce his laws. But his laws and his enforcement contribute in no way to his own private emolument: It is the social body that draws the benefit and profit of his rule. It is to their own true good that he directs the citizens.

Tyrants are legion, kings few, but Jesus of Nazareth is king *par excellence.*

He is king, first, by right of the hypostatic union. This man is king because this man is God; as man, He participates in the dominion of God.

He is king, too, by right of His passion: He has redeemed us, bought us back. By right of purchase we are His to be ruled.

Himself full of grace and truth, He rules by truth and grace.

"Thou sayest that I am a king," was His response to Pilate. "For this I came into the world, that I might give testimony to the truth." On the Mount, in the boat, in the synagogues, and in the temple, He taught the truth by which He directs His subjects to that eternal life that is the good of His kingdom.

He teaches the truth, but His rule ends not with this. We need to accept that truth and make it our own if we are to live by it, and this He takes care of. "He who is of the truth hears my voice," He continues in His discussion with Pilate. Surprising it is that being of the truth precedes hearing His voice, but that is the way of it. Believe, and you are of the truth. Faith is necessary to hear His word, and faith is His gift.

---

[2]*On the Gospel of St. John*, Tractate 51; cf. Roman Breviary, Feast of Christ the King, Matins, 3rd Nocturn, Homily of St. Augustine, Bishop.

But it is not enough that we know the true and the good. We choose and act according to what we love, and so our hearts have to be right, too — no easy matter for fallen man. "It is not that we have first loved God, but that He has first loved us," writes St. John.[3] With the grace He won for us on Calvary, the Lord Christ pours charity into our hearts. Aided and abetted by this gift from above, we can begin to love God as we ought, and our neighbor; to order our lives and our acts to God; and to love the path and the gate that lead to God, rough though the path may be, and narrow the gate.

And so our King's mode of rule is unique; not by constraint from without, but gently, from within, does He rule. By grace and the life of faith and charity poured into our hearts He moves us, His subjects, to God who is our common good. In such a way does He move us that our actions spring at the same time from Him and from the love of our hearts; they are His, but so that they can be rightly called our own.

"Thy kingdom come," we pray in the prayer He gave us.[4] King by right He is, seated at the right hand of the Father. Yet millions there are who acknowledge not His kingdom, and their name is legion who are dedicated to its destruction on earth. But our prayer is not in vain; our prayer is that, moved by His grace, His kingdom may come in their regard — that under the gentle influence of His saving grace they may become of their own wills His subjects. For they are going to become His subjects finally — if not now, willingly, then in the end under the crushing weight of His punishment.

May His kingdom come more perfectly, too, in the hearts of us who profess to follow the King. For ourselves, we pray that He move us to conform our own desires ever more to the good that He wills for us, that His interests and concerns in our own regard and our neighbor's may become ever more our concerns until that day when we reign with Him in the perfect union of mind and will that is the kingdom of heaven.

---

[3] 1 Jn 4:10.   [4] Lk 11:2.

CONVOCATION

47

OUR LORD AS TEACHER

(John 8:32)

School has begun again. The long, demanding year with its unend-ing round of labors — and often very discouraging labors they are — stretches before us. I think that at this time we should take much encouragement from the realization that no other profession has been raised to the level of dignity that ours has been. After all, the Son of God became man only once. During that one life He worked in public only three years. During those three years this is what He was, first and fore-most — a teacher.

He taught the common people. He taught them in the temple and in the cities; He taught them on the hillside and from the boat. When not engaged in teaching the multitudes, He was giving His most intense private courses of instruction to His special students, the Apostles. For these were to carry on His work and needed to know so much more and understand so much more deeply than the rest.

He was good at it — the greatest of teachers. But still He knew the heartbreaking disappointment of not being understood, of lessons not learned. After His Eucharistic sermon, the crowds left Him. After all His insistence on true moral worth as opposed to the opinions of the crowds, James and John still thought the world's judgments about first place made a difference. And the Apostles, after three years under His tutelage, persisted in thinking that first place at table really mattered. At the end, He was forced to chide Philip for not grasping that He and the Father were one.[1]

---

[1]cf. Jn 6:66; Mk 10:37; Lk 22:24; Jn 14:9.

Our Lord Himself was very explicit about the primacy of His work as a teacher. "I have come that you may know the truth," He said, "and the truth may make you free." The free person is the opposite of the slave. Ignorance is slavery because the ignorant person is at the mercy of any Joe that comes down the pike peddling an opinion. The freedom of right judgment — the freedom that comes from knowing the truth and being able to judge in the light of that truth — this is the freedom that Our Divine Lord proclaimed He came to bring.

Like our Master before us, by our work in the classroom we strive to engender that same freedom. Hard work it is, and we are obliged so far as in us lies to be good at it, as our Master was good at it. But a great and worthy work it is, too — as is evident from the time and effort the Son of God Himself put into it.

48

TRUTH AND FREEDOM

(John 8:32)

St. Thomas Aquinas, in the section of the Tertia Pars of the *Summa Theologiae* devoted to the life of Christ, raises a question about the type or kind of life that Christ, Our Lord, led while He was on earth.[1] In the first article he poses the question whether it was fitting that the Lord Christ have led the kind of life He actually did lead — a public life, mingling with the throngs in the temple and in the synagogue, being found in the company of publicans and sinners, teaching the crowds, disputing with the scribes and Pharisees. The alternative might be, for example, the life of a hermit or a recluse. It might just have been more fitting for Christ to have lived so. After all, the Son of God, we might say, should have led the best possible sort of human life. We do hold that the highest and best form is the intellectual life, and this does call for more than a little solitude.

St. Thomas gives his answer as follows: The Son of God became man only once; He led only one public life. That life lasted, to the best of our understanding, somewhere around three years. For that period He was primarily and principally a teacher: "I have come to give testimony to the truth." He taught the high and the low; He taught the crowds and bestowed special tutoring on His chosen twelve. He taught, without much success, the priests of the people. He taught in the synagogues and on the hillsides, on the shore, and even from a boat. St. John makes special note of the first time He taught in the temple of Jerusalem. Teacher's disappointments He knew full well: "O slow to learn," He chided His disciples.[2]

---

[1]IIIa, q. 40.   [2]Mt 15:16.

And He complained to the Jews: "I speak to you and you believe not ... you do not believe because you are not of my sheep."[3]

Even the wonders He wrought served His teaching. They played the role of a middle term, so to speak, to prove the truth of what He taught. "If you do not believe me, then believe the signs."[4]

Our Savior is clear enough on the goal, or purpose, of that teaching to which He dedicated His human life: "I have come that you may know the truth," He proclaimed to those Jews that believed in Him, "and the truth may make you free."

Our contemporary world sees no connection between truth and freedom: the free person is simply the one who defies the rest and follows his impulse of the moment — no learning required. But Our Savior explicitly does affirm such a connection: "The truth may make you free."

Divine Wisdom knew whereof He spoke. A head of cabbage cannot choose, and neither can King, the dog. Neither the vegetable nor the animal can direct its own life along its own chosen path. But we human creatures, created in the image and likeness of God, can and must choose. We have to direct the course of our own lives. But I can claim to be truly a free person to the extent that I am really so self-directed, not enslaved by my lower impulses and appetites, not a slave to the persuasions of any and every Joe that comes down the pike peddling a specious opinion.

But ignorance means slavery, and I can't be really self-directed unless I know something. I have to know what my true and God-given goal really is, as a human being. I have to know, at least in a general way, by what sort of life, what way of life, that goal is to be attained. In the light of such truth serenely possessed, I can be free; I can direct my own life along the right paths to the right goal. Without such knowledge I can only be a slave to my passions, or to any talker who is glibber than I. "The truth may make you free," says the Lord Christ. He is not guaranteeing that it will, but the miraculous aside, there is no genuine freedom without some knowledge of the truth, quietly, serenely, and permanently possessed, to direct ourselves by.

[3] Jn 10:25–26.　[4] Jn 10:38.

Such a body of knowledge is not easy to come by; we are certainly not born with it. If it is to be gained at all, this is through that course of studies termed liberal, a liberal education — a program named from its goal, which is to make men truly *liberi*, free.

We are about to dedicate another year to such education. We are about to bend our efforts to obtain and possess the truth that contributes so mightily to true human liberty, so precious for ourselves as individuals and for our nation as a whole. It is an arduous quest, but we have the Lord's testimony it is an indispensable one — without knowledge of the truth, genuine human freedom must ever elude us. We begin with prayerful acknowledgement of our dependence on God's help in the quest undertaken. We begin without anxiety and with complete tranquility and with a sense of joy at something worthwhile about to be accomplished and gained. We begin with sincerity, moreover, and a deep awareness of the urgency of the task at hand.

FEASTS THROUGHOUT THE ACADEMIC YEAR

49

NORTH AMERICAN MARTYRS

For the past few years, October 19 — which, of course, was yesterday — has been in the Church the feast day of the North American Martyrs. For decades previous this same feast had been celebrated on September 26, a day of no small solemnity in Jesuit houses. When the date was changed, this came as something of a wrench, like changing the feast of St. Thomas from March 7 to January 28. It strikes us as almost a violation of the natural law.

The Collect prayer of yesterday's Mass mentions the North American martyrs simply as Isaac, John, and their companions, or if you happen to be in Canada, then John, Isaac, and their companions. The liturgy makes no mention, as it has no reason to, that they were French by birth and nationality, that they were eight in number, that six were Jesuit priests and the other two, at the time of their deaths, brothers in this same least Society.

The Collect prayer mentions North America as the place where these saints labored and died. It defines the locale no more precisely than that. Actually, what is now central New York State was the site of Father Jogues' labors and death, his and the two Brothers René Goupil and John Lalande. The western sector of the present Canadian province of Ontario, along the eastern shore of Lake Huron around the present town of Midland, is where Brébeuf and Lalemant, Daniel, Garnier, and Chabanel labored and died.

In New York State, about forty miles west of the state capital, along the south bank of the Mohawk river in the wide valley that divides the Catskill mountains to the south from the Adirondacks to the north, is the small village, not much more than a post office, of Auriesville. A few miles to the east, sloping upward from the south bank of the river, are several acres that the Jesuits have owned now for many decades. They call it the Auriesville Shrine, and it is a pilgrimage center for Catholics of the Northeast. The Jesuits built a shrine there, a large dodecahedron with seventy-two doors, a bit of a monstrosity in fact. But it really doesn't matter much. It is not the building that sanctifies that portion of real estate; what Father Jogues suffered and did there hallowed that spot far beyond the power of future generations to add or subtract.

One walks the paths among the trees there even today and one has the sense of being in a sanctuary or walking on sacred ground, ground hallowed some three hundred and forty years ago by the priest who spent thirteen months there as a captive of the Mohawk Indians, literally a slave of the savages. It is ground sanctified, more precisely, by the patience and perseverance with which he endured pain and privation there, by the quiet persistent energy with which he went about doing what he could for the salvation of souls, by the love of Our Lord and Savior Jesus Christ, which motivated it all.

Father Jogues was brought in bonds to that spot on the Mohawk, a captive of the Indians after whom the stream is named. A war party took him in ambush far to the north, in the French country along the St. Lawrence, and brought him to their homeland. There was one with him named René Goupil, whom Father Jogues received into the Society of Jesus as a brother, and who died soon after at Auriesville of a hatchet blow. Goupil was the first of the martyrs.

Father Jogues was enslaved there along the Mohawk, suffered there, did what he could there, baptizing the dying, for thirteen months. With the help of the Dutch at Albany, he escaped and returned to France. He received permission from Pope Urban to say Mass with what was left of his mangled hands, and at his own request returned to the missions in New France.

The Iroquois were seeking peace now, or at least pretended to be, with the French and all things French. They would welcome Father Jogues back among them as a goodwill ambassador. With misgivings, but moved by hope of some missionary success, he begged to be allowed to return to the site of his former agonies. For the second time, but now of his own free choice, he took his place in the Iroquois canoe and headed toward Mohawk. Again there was a brother with him — John Lalande. That was in July 1646.

The Iroquois change of heart proved to be not much more than another instance of savage treachery, and on October 18 of that year, a blow of a tomahawk sent him home. The following day John Lalande met the same fate.

To the extent that we acquire any familiarity with the lives of the martyrs, we live in admiration of their incredible patience and fortitude; their unbelievable endurance in the midst of the filth and squalor in diet and abode; the undisguised and unconcealed immorality and the insensitivity and unspeakable brutality of man to man in which they took it upon themselves to live. They reported it all to their superiors back home, as they were bidden to do. In the hundreds of pages of the *Jesuit Relations* there are many requests for prayerful assistance but never a whimper, never a complaint. In all their writings there shines forth the portrait of the most beautiful things under heaven — utterly unselfish men.

In the accomplishment of their own work they were pros. They knew what they were about. Along Georgian Bay, among the more receptive Hurons, they worked with no small success. They learned the dialects and compiled dictionaries. They taught the savages to read and taught them the rudiments of healthy living. They improved the farming methods and increased their vocabularies so they could be instructed about the Trinity and the Incarnation, the fall, and grace and the sacraments. They made solid converts in ever-increasing numbers. Gradually their stockade villages became kernels of Christian civilization, with Church and school at the center.

Over it all there hung an air of impermanence and the near certainty of ultimate failure because of the ever-present threat from the

south. For the Iroquois, their war against the Hurons was a war of exter-
mination. When the trails became passable in the spring, the war parties
headed north, and the Hurons were no match for them. The Jesuits in
Huronia were too well aware of the kind of end that awaited them — it
was just a question of time.

The final destruction both of themselves and their work came in
1648 and 1649. For some, death was mercifully swift. Father Daniel fell
in a shower of arrows; Chabanel and Garnier took blows of the hatchet.
But John de Brébeuf and Gabriel Lalemant were captured together.
Brébeuf was five hours at the stake. Lalemant's turn followed, and the
savages prolonged his agony from sunset to sunrise. The two men
endured every pain that knife and flame and boiling water can inflict, but
in the end they conquered their conquerors, for there was never a whimper or a scream on the lips of either, only the prayer of Christ: "Father,
forgive them."

"O God, who have consecrated the first fruits of North America by
the preaching and the blood of Isaac and John and their companions,"
we pray in the Collect prayer of the Mass. The history of this country
and Canada was sanctified, consecrated, and hallowed at its source by
the sufferings and deaths, successes and failures, of eight very great men.
After this introduction in the opening prayer, the Church makes its petition — a petition for the continuation on earth of that work to which they
dedicated their lives: "Grant that through their intercession the flowering
harvest of Christians may be increased every day and everywhere."

50

ALL SAINTS

(Revelation 7:2–4, 9–14; Matthew 5:1–12)

In the entrance hymn of this day's Mass, the Church commends to us who are still engaged in the struggle for our eternal salvation, to "rejoice in the Lord" and "keep a festival in honor of all the saints."

We have our own personal reason for rejoicing on the festival of the saints, for thanks to them we have a holiday — all the sweeter for being the first one of the academic year.

But it is the reason mentioned in the entrance hymn that is the principal one for the gladness of the day, and the Church's reason, and the unselfish one.

For the Church would have us rejoice in the great good of others — others who are, in fact, testimonials to God's grace and the wonders that that grace can accomplish. They are others not alien to us, not separated from us, but fellow members of the same Mystical Body of Christ, the Church triumphant.

"The souls of the just are in the hands of God," says the Book of Wisdom.[1] God has poured His grace into their hearts through the Spirit that is given to them, and that grace has not been given in vain. Through it, no matter what, though the way of failure may have marked their lives, they have succeeded simply. For them the battle is over and won; the time of faith and hope is followed by vision face to face and joy beyond the mind of man to conceive. "These are the ones who have survived the great period of trial; they have washed their robes and made them white in the blood of the Lamb." The Church would have us be glad

---

[1]Wis 3:1.

169

because of that joy which, through the grace and mercy of God, the saints have earned.

With the Church, we pray to them all today. We honor them for the only glory worthy of the name, the only glory that lasts, the glory of saintliness. They are the masterpieces of God's grace. They have won the approbation of the only one whose approbation has ever meant anything, Christ, Our Lord: "Come, ye blessed of my Father, into the kingdom prepared for you."[2]

Through them the Lord God has provided us with examples we can love and follow. In their number are exemplars of Christian heroism, an inspiration to ourselves and the rest of the world, the glory of our race, and the proof that it can be done.

With humility we acknowledge their holiness; with humility we praise them for having loved God and their fellow man more than we have, for having been more Christ-like than we have been, for having done greater things than we have done, for having taken seriously Our Savior's injunctions on the Mount: "Blessed are the poor in spirit … the sorrowing … those who hunger and thirst after justice … who are persecuted for holiness' sake." All have shared in the passion of Christ in some particular way; they have drunk deeply of the chalice of which He drank. "In the eyes of the foolish they seemed to die," says the Book of Wisdom, "but they are at peace."[3]

It is for our own good, too, that the Church would have us rejoice this day: the glory of the saints is not divorced from our own. The vast army of the blessed, present before the throne of God, are a boon inestimable for us who still have to ask ourselves daily: "How am I doing? How goes the battle?" St. Thomas Aquinas, in his long question on prayer in the *Secunda Secundae*, inquires "whether those who are *in patria*, in the homeland, pray for us."[4]

He answers his own question in the affirmative and gives his reason: It is from charity that prayer for others flows. Where the heart is full of love, prayer for others flows easily, with joy and abundance, and this our own experience confirms. Charity evokes prayer for those in need thereof; intense charity is an abundant font of the same. But the "*sancti*

---

[2]Mt 25:34.   [3]Wis 3:2–3.   [4]IIaIIae, q. 83, a. 11.

qui sunt in patria sunt perfectioris caritatis" — the saints who are in the homeland are more perfect in charity. They are crowned as they are precisely because of the depth and the breadth of the charity that is theirs. From such love they pray for us who are still on the way, who stand in no small need of their prayer.

Not only do they pray for us then, but the saint adds that because of the closeness of their union with God, their prayers are all the more efficacious. In them we have, together with Christ Himself at their head, most powerful intercessors before the throne of glory. And so the Church has always commended to Christ's followers that they pray to God through the saints, and so in fact we do in the Collect prayer itself of this day's Mass: "Today we rejoice in the holy men and women of every time and place. May their prayers bring us your forgiveness and love."

51

ALL SOULS

(Wisdom 3:1–9; John 11:21–27)

In the liturgy of this day, the Church displaces the Mass of the thirty-first Sunday, substituting in its place the Mass for All Souls Day. Clearly the Church would have us on this day call to mind the souls of the faithful departed and renew our fervent prayers for those who suffer in Purgatory — or may be there suffering — the souls especially of those who were dear and close to us during their days on earth.

It is traditional, a familiar custom in the Church, that the month of November be dedicated to those souls called holy — holy because their last moments on earth, their last moments to merit or demerit, found them united with God, secure in His grace: "The souls of the just are in the hands of God," we read in the Book of Wisdom — yet still in His debt. The time is not yet that they should abide with Him in heaven. ("You shall not be released until you have paid the last farthing."[1])

Prayer is effective. Man at prayer actually does accomplish things, as Our Savior made clear to us. It is the doctrine of the Church that we actually do help the holy souls by our prayers; thus the increase of sincere and earnest prayer hour by hour and day by day during the thirty days of this month is the behest of the Church.

This day is one of two days in the liturgical year on which it is granted to each priest to offer three Masses. The Church itself has composed three different Masses for the day, of which we are at the moment reading the first. Its theme, obviously enough, is the resurrection. The Mass, like the preface of the dead, would have us focus our thoughts

[1]Mt 5:26

on the overwhelming truth of our faith: death for Christ was not final. His enemies exulted that they were through once and for all with that imposter — but on the third day He arose to a new life, free from all touch of pain or fret, free of evil or anxiety, the kind of life we all dream about.

As it was for the Master, so it will be for the disciple: Christ, St. Paul tells his Christians of Corinth, is the first fruits of those who have fallen asleep.[2] The faithful Christian who follows Him in bearing His cross in this mortal life will follow Him also in the life of glory, alive again. Therefore we profess in the preface of the Mass, "The sadness of death gives way to the bright promise of immortality. Lord, for your faithful, life is changed, not ended."

In the passage from St. John which we read just a few moments ago, Martha spoke the truth when she affirmed that her brother would arise on the last day. Our Savior's response is causal in its character: "I am the resurrection and the life" — words that seem mysterious enough, but they make sense if we understand them in terms of cause. He is the resurrection of all, as cause thereof.

By His agony, His death, His resurrection, He is the cause meritorious of the resurrection of all unto glory. His own body, gloriously risen from the dead, stands as exemplar for all: "From heaven will come the Lord Christ," says the Apostle, "and He will transform these wretched bodies of ours into images of His own glorious body."[3]

"I am the resurrection and the life" — resurrection because the life. Himself "full of grace and truth," as St. John proclaims Him,[4] He is the source for all others of that grace that is the life of their souls, and through their souls of their glorified bodies.

For the eternal and glorified life of which this Mass reminds us, we most sincerely and earnestly hope. This hope, which must never die, we rest not on our own moral fiber, not on our own good will, not on our strength of character. These always prove unsteady. We rest our hope rather on the love and mercy of God, from which flows forgiveness without end, from which flows strength supernatural, which we call grace, to persevere in His way of life. And the sign and proof of this boundless

---

[2] 1 Cor 15:20.   [3] Phil 3:20–21.   [4] Jn 11:25; Jn 1:14.

mercy and love is that Christ died for us: "When we were still powerless," writes the Apostle, "Christ died for us godless men … It is precisely in this that God proved His love for us, that while we were still sinners, Christ died for us."[5]

---

[5]Rom 5:6, 8.

52

SAINT JOHN LATERAN

(Genesis 28:10–17; 1 Corinthians 3:9–11, 16–17; Luke 19:1–10)

Today, in the calendar of the Church, *qua* Sunday, it is the thirty-second in Ordinary Time. But this same day, *qua* November 9, celebrates the dedication of a particular Roman basilica — the basilica of St. John Lateran, a church that enjoys a certain pre-eminence in the Catholic world. It is the cathedral, for one thing, of the Pope as Bishop of Rome; for another, on the grounds of this basilica, throughout the middle ages stood the palace and the church that were to the world during those centuries what the Vatican is to us today. So we are enjoined to read this day not the Mass of the Sunday, but the Mass of the dedication.

From the liturgical selections it seems to be the Church's intention, on the occasion of this anniversary, to direct our attention to the treasure that is actually ours in any one of our Catholic churches, to reawaken our appreciation of our church buildings because they are, *par excellence*, the house of God.

In the Old Testament selection we find Jacob, alone, passing a night at some sort of shrine or another, a stone for a pillow. He dreams an unforgettable dream. In some way or other, the Lord God makes His presence known to him, addresses him, and makes him the beneficiary of a magnificent promise. Then when Jacob awakens, he sees his surroundings as different — as holy in a way that other places were not, holy in a way in which it was not at this time yesterday. "How awesome is this shrine" is his reflection. "This is nothing else but an abode of God." True enough, but we have news for Jacob. Through His Son Incarnate, the

Lord God has wrought, in these New Testament times, wonders of which the Patriarchs could never have dreamt. For these walls, within which we at this moment gather, form indeed the abode of the Lord in a real and permanent way, which it could not have entered into the heart of Jacob to conceive. Holy is this place with a holiness of which the Holy of Holies was no more than a figure.

The Gospel selection from St. Luke's nineteenth chapter is the warm and charming story of the half-pint Zacchaeus, who wasn't dreaming. Zacchaeus was by profession what the Jews of Our Lord's day loathed about as much as they detested the Samaritans: an internal revenue agent in the employ of Rome; not just a revenuer, but a chief among the revenuers. One might surmise, moreover, from the little man's generous pledge of restitution that his remarkable wealth was not come by all that honestly: "If I have defrauded anyone in the least, I pay him back fourfold." He might not have been entirely above a little honest graft, or perhaps even loansharking or something of the sort.

In any case, when he arose that particular morning, the little man had no way to suspect that this was to be a red-letter day in his life. He must have appeared at least a little ridiculous in his attempts to see what Jesus was like. A grown man, he first "ran out in front," says St. Luke, and when that didn't work, he climbed a sycamore tree which was along Jesus' route.

His efforts to catch a glimpse of the Lord Christ by climbing a tree paid off handsomely. He discovered that not even he, outcast and sinner though he may have been, is beyond the scope of Christ's loving concern. For the Lord Christ, source of all goodness, looked up and entered into his life that day. "Zacchaeus, make haste and come down, for I must stay at your house today."

There is a consoling side to this episode. Let no one despair; let no one ever suppose that God has done with him, that his last chance is spent, that the road ahead must go down and ever down; let not the striving man of faith imagine that because he prayed so poorly today he will pray poorly tomorrow.

"Today is salvation come to this house." The concern of Our Savior for Zacchaeus can convert our pessimism about ourselves into a kind of optimism, an optimism founded on nothing that is in us, but on the mercy of Christ, the mercy of God.

Be that as it may, the Church would seem to have her own particular reasons for focusing our attention on Our Savior's encounter with Zacchaeus at the Gospel of a Mass commemorating the dedication of a church. "I mean to stay in your house." The Incarnate Word, who in this life had not whereon to lay His head, made Zacchaeus' house literally the House of God for a day or so. From that day forward the publican's dwelling was holy in a way that it was not before.

Yet for all that, Zacchaeus' house is at best a figure of this, our own chapel. Christ, man and God, is here present not for but a day, but day and night, month after month. Our building is holy indeed — holy because God herein dwells in a way in which He is not elsewhere; holy because herein is the principal source of our own holiness, Christ to whom we pray and who is the Eucharist that nourishes the life of the soul. The Christian people receive worthily, rightly, the body of Christ, and the life of grace flourishes in them.

Where grace is, therein, in another special way, God dwells. We have Our Savior's own word for this, recorded in St. John's fourteenth chapter: "If any man loves me, my Father will love him, and I will love him, and we will come to him and take up our abode with him."[1]

In this temple we become, and remain, ourselves temples of God. Of this the Apostle reminds the Christians of Corinth, as we heard in this day's second reading. "Are you not aware that you are temples of God and that the Spirit of God dwells in you?" And it is in accord with this reminder from the Apostle that we pray in the Mass' opening prayer: "God, Our Father … increase the spiritual gifts you have given your Church, that your faithful may continue to grow into the new and eternal Jerusalem."

[1] cf. Jn 14:21, 23.

53
XAVIER

Today in the calendar of the Church is the first Sunday of Advent. But also insofar as it is December 3, it is the feast day, and has been now for 356 years, of Saint Francis Xavier. The time has come for a Jesuit commercial.

Time was, not too long ago, when schools and the pulpits paid more heed and honor to the saints than now; in the churches there were more devotions to the saints than now; and Catholics in general were more familiar with Christ's great ones than they are today. The statement may have been true then which a gentleman in Boston made to me once: "St. Francis is everybody's favorite."

The body that the saint drove so mercilessly is to this day incorrupt, sealed away in the city of Goa in southwest India, which was his base. In 1949, his severed right arm was brought on a coast-to-coast tour of this country, and some ten million people were reckoned to have come to the churches to view that arm and so pay homage to the missionary extraordinary, the apostle of all the East. The sheer magnitude of the enterprise he undertook for the love of Christ staggers the imagination and captures the admiration of men.

He was a Basque by birth, from Navarre, in the part of Spain bordering on the Pyrenees and France. In the late 1520s he was a student at the University of Paris, ambitious for glory on earth, not the least interested in sanctity or the service of Christ. But there came limping into his life another Basque, Ignatius from Loyola, older than he, already well on his way to that heroic sanctity that characterized his mature years.

What Ignatius discerned in Francis at that stage to make him worth a siege lasting nearly three years is hidden from us. But deep calls to deep, and a great heart is quick to recognize its fellow, even under veils.

Xavier's dreams had been his own dreams — success, fame, the credit of a great name on earth. One breach after another Ignatius, the patient besieger, made in Francis' defenses. Ignatius bided his time, watched for a sortie of pride, and then flung his question: "Francis, what does it profit a man if he gain the whole world and suffer the loss of his soul?" Finally, the ambitions of Francis Xavier returned — reversed — ambitions now not for himself but for the glory of Christ, Our Lord, and on that day all the bells of heaven rang.

Five others, devout men and zealous, joined themselves to Ignatius and Xavier, and the seven pronounced vows at Montmartre in August 1534. In 1540, when their numbers had grown to some thirteen and Ignatius had drawn up constitutions, Pope Paul III formally approved the Society of Jesus as a religious order existing in the Church.

The following year King John of Portugal requested Ignatius to send a papal legate to Portugal's new empire in India. Xavier was the man, and on April 7, 1541, his thirty-fifth birthday, he sailed from Lisbon. There began then a decade of the most courageous and tireless missionary enterprise this world has ever seen.

On shipboard and in the harbors, never for a minute did Xavier leave off hearing confessions, teaching Christian doctrine, tending the sick, and all this in joy.

He was a man consumed with a divine impatience, a saint in a hurry. Sometimes he has been accused of restlessness, but God knows, as he would say himself, that his vagabondage was not due to an itch for change or a desire for more interesting labors. He "must go to open doors," he said, and God knows too what each door cost him in privation and suffering. If he spent only five months in Goa when he first arrived there, they were at any rate months never to be forgotten by the sick, the poor, the slaves, the outcasts, the half-baked converts from heathenism among whom he labored day and night.

During his decade in the East, Xavier's trademark was his bell. In the city's churches he preached in Portuguese, itself a foreign tongue to him, but apart from that his worst trouble was the native languages. He would have someone translate the prayers and commandments for him into Tamil, or whatever. In his own words, "When I had them fixed in my memory, I went through the whole place with my bell in my hand, gathering all the boys and men that I could, and teaching them twice a day for a month." Xavier has been falsely credited with the gift of tongues, and one can understand why; but one might also wonder if that month's toil were not itself a lovelier miracle than any gift of tongues would have been.

"So great is the multitude which turns to the faith in this land where I wander," he wrote to St. Ignatius, "that often my arms are weary with baptizing, and I have no voice left through so frequently reciting the Creed and the commandments." A short while later his arms must have been almost paralyzed, for up and down the dreary, inhospitable land of Tranvacore, he baptized in the course of a single month more than ten thousand persons. Taking a twelve-hour day, that would have been about one baptism every two minutes for thirty days consecutively.

Beyond India, Malacca beckoned, and beyond Malacca, the Moluccas and the Spice Islands. Three of his brethren came to take up his burden in India, so by September 1545 he had crossed two thousand miles of perilous seas to his goal. There he labored in his usual style in the city of Malacca, chiefly among the Portuguese colonists who needed converting no less than did the native Malays. From there it was to the jungles of Amboina and the Moro Islands, from which he was not to be deterred by the consideration that the islanders were headhunters.

In the spring of 1547 it was back to Malacca. There he first heard of Japan, where the name of Christ was altogether unknown and no word of the Gospel yet preached, where, in fact, no European had as yet penetrated. In April 1549 he left from Goa on his six thousand mile voyage to

Japan, knowing of course not a word of Japanese. His years there were, in one word, disappointment.

"In Cape Comorin," as one of his fellow Jesuits expressed it, "he had fished with a net, but in Japan he was obliged to fish with a line." He was persecuted by the rulers, the people, the children, the weather. In all, Japan was heartbreak. In mid-November 1551 he sailed from Japan, leaving behind, after about two-and-a-half years labor there in Kagoshima, Ichiu, Yamaguchi, Hirado, Fujimi, no more than two thousand Christians — very few out of a population of some fifteen million. God, however, does not count by numbers, and from this little flock at a later time came one of the Church's greatest regiments of its white-robed army of martyrs.

India, the East Indies, the Spice Islands, Japan — all this was not big enough for his great heart. There was still China. To enter China in those days, he would have to be smuggled in. In the late summer of 1552 he reached the smuggler's paradise of San Cian, a barren and empty island off the Cantonese coast. He waited there until he found a Chinese trader who agreed to smuggle him into the mainland. The day was set for November 19.

That day dawned. His books and his little bundle of clothes beside him, Francis waited, watching the shore. Hour after hour he waited. There was nothing to see, not a sign of the brown sail he had hoped for. Then he knew that China had beaten him, and the poor body, so long driven by the dauntless spirit, took its revenge. At that moment he fell ill. A fortnight later, the night of December 2, 1552, he was dead, forty-six years and seven months old. He whose hand had been raised in absolution countless times died without a priest within a thousand miles of him and was buried without ceremony in a deserted island in unhallowed ground.

Just seventy years later, on March 12, Pope Gregory XV raised to the altar the two who were such fast friends on earth — Ignatius and Xavier. Pope Pius X declared St. Francis patron of the Propagation of the Faith and of all Catholic missions.

In all, he voyaged some seventy-five thousand miles, three

circumnavigations of the globe. He spent a total of two full years on ship-board — and we are not talking about the Queen Mary. The distance from Goa to Cape Comorin is roughly New York to Miami. Xavier trav-elled it thirteen times, either on foot or in the rickety, leaky, creaking tubs that passed for boats in those climes.

If we expect Francis to provide us with a diary of his voyaging, we do not know him at all. He had his own interests, but they were centered so exclusively on men's souls that in his 127 extant letters, written close by jungles and perilous seas, not a single elephant trumpets, not a tiger roars, not a shark shows a fin. His letters are marked by scrambled gram-mar, atrocious spelling, boring repetitions, and thoughts that burn like flames. In all, there shines forth the portrait of the most beautiful thing under heaven: the totally unselfish man.

54

THE WONDROUS LEARNING OF BLESSED THOMAS

We are come together here at the Holy Sacrifice of the Mass this afternoon to commemorate the death of this school's patron. The death of so great, so holy a man, who served the Church of Christ in so signal a fashion, is indeed an occasion not only to commemorate, but even more to celebrate. For it marks the occasion of the Saint's hearing from the lips of Him whom he had so loved and served, "Well done, thou good and faithful servant, enter into the joy of the Lord." As the Alleluia verse proclaims in his Mass, "The Lord has loved him and adorned him, and laid on him a stole of glory."

According to the second nocturn of the old office of St. Thomas, he did indeed die on the seventh of March in 1274. Pope Gregory X had sent him as theologian to the Council of Lyons. But the Council had to face and solve its problems without him, at least without his actual physical presence. En route, his final illness laid hold of him, and he died among the Cistercian monks in their monastery at Fossa Nova.

It is symbolic of the indefatigable industry that characterized his entire life that, ill though he was, he spent his last days at work — on the Canticle of Canticles. These final labors are indicative still more of the depth of the love of God which moved him, even then in those days of failing energies, to deepen by just a little his understanding of God's word contained in that Old Testament allegory and to transmit to the monks about him the divine truth so discovered.

The Collect prayers of the Mass — which we call now the open-ing prayers — have a way of beginning with an acknowledgment, end-ing with a petition. In this respect the prayer of St. Thomas' old Mass runs true to form: "O God, who dost enlighten your Church with the wondrous learning of Blessed Thomas …" It is God Himself, so runs our acknowledgment, who has been at work in His Church through the genius and the labors and the prayerfulness of Thomas Aquinas.

The Divine work alluded to is just that — a work of enlightenment; we acknowledge that God "dost enlighten …" Man needs light. In the dark we are unsure; the dark offers concealment for the forces of evil who love to work therein. We need light to live by, to direct our steps aright.

This light, we profess, this needed light, God has granted His Church. He has bestowed it *"mira eruditione beati Thomae,"* by the learn-ing of St. Thomas that is wondrous, far beyond the ordinary, as learned men go. He has left us that learning, and we find it is marvelous, for example, in its universality, unmatched in this regard by any other. For St. Thomas knew well all of nature, at least on the universal plane, and man, especially, who is nature's crown — his senses and emotions, his mind and will. And his learning extends to nature's first cause, God one and three, to the Incarnation and redemption, the law and grace and the Church, morality and the religious life, prayer. This same doctrine is marvelous, too, in its depth. For the resolution is where it ought to be — into self-evident principles or the revealed word of God. As that same learning came from his pen, it is no less marvelous in the precision and conciseness, the serenity and tranquil assurance of its expression. The language in which he speaks is itself a work of art in which no art is apparent; it is not possible to improve on his expression of what is to be expressed. Wondrous also is the sheer magnitude of the *Opera Omnia,* completed in the whereabouts of twenty-five years.

In the prayer of the old Mass, our acknowledgment of God's work among us continues: "You enrich your Church by his holy work." Our liturgy is, in concept, to help us turn the thoughts of our minds and the affections of our hearts toward God. What St. Thomas has contributed thereto does just that. The liturgical office of Corpus Christi, for example, is his work. Our hymns to the Blessed Sacrament most treasured for their content and fervor are his: *Pange Lingua, Adoro Te Devote, Lauda Sion, Verbum Supernum.* The prayers of his own heart that he committed to ink and paper can, in turn, help us to pray and to pray well — prayers centered upon the Mass, the Blessed Sacrament, the Mother of God, and the prayer, as we well know, before study.

"O God, who dost enlighten your Church by the wondrous learning and enrich it by the holy work of St. Thomas. . ." On reflection, we are grateful for the brightness and the extent of that enlightenment, dismayed by the thought of the resultant darkness without it.

Then in this same prayer we make our petition. We make of God a request that we make in the Mass of no other Doctor — *"et quae docuit intellectu conspicere"* — to know what he taught, at least as much thereof as opportunity and our own efforts, assisted by the grace of God, will allow.

Clearly the Church would have us take St. Thomas seriously. This brief prayer of the Church finds its echo in the encyclical *Aeterni Patris* of Pope Leo XIII, in which he established St. Thomas as *the* teacher of Christ's followers. This same pontiff named St. Thomas heavenly patron of Catholic schools, colleges, and seminaries. The urging of the authoritative magisterium must constitute our initial motive for a special and unique attention to St. Thomas. This first motive may well, in time, yield to another — a conviction born of experience. We follow the Church's direction and come to find that she is right. St. Thomas never fails, and never disappoints. The effort required to grasp what he has said is not small in many matters, but then neither are the rewards. For he provides us with knowledge that not only directs toward happiness in this life and in the life to come, but itself makes happy and constitutes a foretaste of the Blessed Vision to come.

BACCALAUREATE

55

THE PARACLETE

(Acts 2:1–11; John 14:15–16, 23–26)

Reverend Fathers, graduates, members of the faculty, parents, relatives and friends of the graduates:

We have come here to this campus this morning, from near or far
as the case may be, to share with our graduates their joy on this day when
they receive into their hands proof positive, legal, and binding that they
have here completed a course of collegiate studies — including a senior
thesis and the anxiety that goes with it — and so won their place in the
community of scholars.

The day is not without its shadows. A worthwhile way of life is
about to end; so too is the cherished company of good friends.

Yet the cause for joy is truly at hand, for these young men and
women have accomplished a work of no small difficulty and of no small
worth. They have persevered, and they have succeeded. The diploma they
are soon to receive from the hand of His Excellency will bear witness that
they have here learned truths of some moment and so thereby grown
in the likeness of God who knows all things. Theirs now is a kind of
learning which, did it thrive more commonly across these United States,
would alter in no insignificant way the face of this land of ours.

By dint of a certain labor inside of class and out, they have acquired
some light whereby they can judge — and judge rightly — of the true
and the false, the good and the bad. They are not apt to be beguiled or
allured by the hollow, the specious, or the empty, and their learning is
the basis of that genuine self-direction in which true human freedom

finally consists. "I have come that you may know the truth," said the Lord Christ, "and the truth may make you free."[1] So to have learned is no small reason for joy.

We are at this moment engaged in an essential and momentous part of the graduation ceremonies. We are here before this altar united in spirit to offer this Mass. With the graduates and for them we offer again the sacrifice of Calvary, the worship of our Catholic religion. There is no way more fitting to render to Almighty God our thanks for the graces of these last four years; there is no way more efficacious to beg of the Lord God His light and strength for these graduates in the new and quite different lives that now open before them.

Twice in the course of the school year we here depart from the liturgical order to offer instead the Votive Mass of the Holy Spirit. With this particular liturgy we begin the academic year. September marks once again the inception of the quest for wisdom and the truth that makes free. It is fitting that at that time through the Mass of the Holy Spirit we should invoke the aid of Him who is teacher *par excellence*. "The Paraclete, the Holy Spirit, whom the Father will send in my name, will teach you all things" was Our Savior's promise to His chosen eleven at the Last Supper, "and He will recall to you all I have said to you." And again, says St. John in his first epistle, "His anointing will teach you all things."[2]

With this same Mass of the Holy Spirit we here today close our school year. Here again it is most appropriate that we turn our prayerful attention to the Paraclete and in a manner special and most earnest invoke His aid, not because the occasion marks an end, but rather because here again what we are commemorating is a beginning.

The New Testament reading of this day's Mass, which we read just a few moments ago, recounts the familiar events of the first Pentecost Sunday. The Lord Christ had ascended into heaven, and His disciples were huddled together nervous and uncertain about the future, doubtful and hesitant about the next step. St. Luke recounts the wondrous details — the wind and the fire — but the point is that into that group the Holy Spirit came, and coming, made a difference.

[1] Jn 8:32.   [2] 1 Jn 2:27.

The situation of these young men and women at the moment reflects that Pentecost scene to a degree. A time of security in surroundings, marked by charity and community of lofty purpose, has come to an end; uncertainty in a world for which Christ would not pray, a world indifferent and unsympathetic, opens before them. The occasion calls for the aid of the Holy Spirit and His light; accordingly we invoke Him. If our invocation rests on custom, the custom in turn rests firmly on the truths of our Catholic faith.

"I believe in the Holy Spirit," we profess in the Creed, "the Lord and giver of life." "The giver of life," "the Sanctifier," we call Him. The words are to be taken seriously, for they mean much. That we have a supernatural life that is truly that, this is a truth distinctive of our Catholic faith and proper to it. And it is equally a truth of our faith that this life is owing, in a particular way, to the Spirit.

St. John devotes some four chapters of his Gospel to Christ's final discourse to His chosen eleven immediately following His Last Supper. The occasion was a solemn one and a serious one, and Our Savior spoke of matters of moment. He spoke of the Spirit whom He would send from above: "I will ask the Father and He will give you another Paraclete, that He may abide with you forever ... He shall abide with you and shall be in you." "The Holy Spirit whom the Father will send in my name will teach you all things." "When the Paraclete comes whom I shall send you from the Father, He shall give testimony of me."[3] "It is expedient for you that I go, for if I go not, the Paraclete will not come to you; but if I go, I will send Him to you."[4]

What Our Savior's words point to, finally, is the fact of a friendship between God and man, a friendship whose reality and character, did He not reveal them to us, we could never have suspected. He speaks of an invaluable friendship of which God is the author, a friendship which in a particular way is the work of the Holy Spirit.

"I will send Him and He will abide with you," Our Savior says. We have Eternal Truth's word for it that the Spirit, according to His own way, mysterious as it may be, is really present in the souls where grace abounds. "Know you not that you are temples of the Holy Spirit?" St. Paul

---

[3] Jn 15:26.   [4] Jn 16:7.

asks the Christians of Corinth.[5] Being present, the Spirit must indeed make an inestimable difference.

He proceeds from the Father and the Son, and proceeds as love. Love is His name, as St. Thomas explains in the *Summa*.[6] His first gift to the soul transformed by grace is a love of God of which He Himself is the exemplar and pattern. He makes our own hearts over to His own image; because He is as He is, our charity is as it is — a reality divine in its character. "The charity of God is diffused in our hearts through the Holy Spirit, who is given to us," the Apostle informs the Christians of Rome,[7] and accordingly in the hymn *Veni Sancte Spiritus*, we address this Spirit: *Dulcis hospes animae* — welcome guest of the soul.

That we so love God, with a love divine and not human, is His gift to us, but then God returns love for love: "I love those who love me," we read in the Book of Proverbs.[8]

But mutual love, recognized, is the heart and soul of friendship, and so Our Savior in view of this union of God and man that is the Spirit's work informs His Apostles, "I call you not now servants, but friends."[9]

Friends love each other's company. The effect and sign of friendship is constant and close communion, and so the Lord Christ informs His followers, "If any man loves me, he will keep my commandments, and I will love him, and my Father will love him, and we will come to him and take up our abode in him." Our Catholic faith affirms such an indwelling and annuls the Hebrews' boast of old: "No other nation has their God so close to them as our God is to us."[10]

But the beloved dwells in the affections of the friend, and so as God is in us, so we are in Him. "Who remains in charity remains in God and God in him," says St. John in his epistle.[11]

Friend regards his friend as another self and so is willing to forgive; we need forgiveness and can count on our friend for it. For the same reason, friend wills to share with friend the goods that are his own. We have it on divine authority that the charity which is the gift of the Spirit and which is the foundation of this friendship is but the first of His gifts. *Tu septiformis munere* — Thou sevenfold in Thy gifts — we address Him in the Church's song *Veni Creator Spritus*. The wisdom, knowledge,

---

[5] 1 Cor 6:19.   [6] Ia, q. 31, a. 1.   [7] Rom 5:5.   [8] Prov 8:17.   [9] Jn 15:15.   [10] Deut 4:7.
[11] 1 Jn 4:16.

and counsel that are His, He shares, as Our Savior shared His with His friends: "Whatsoever the Father has made known to me, I have revealed to you."[12] Fortitude over the years and fear of the Lord, these we need, and these He bestows. He is the Paraclete, the Advocate, and so we address Him: *Consolator optime* — strengthener *par excellence*. He is the source of our friendship with God and of the goods that count for eternity.

On the first Pentecost Sunday the Spirit came, and being come, made a difference. The fact that His coming does so make a difference, these graduates of ours have themselves acknowledged over the past four years as they began each one of so many classes with the invocation, "Come, Holy Spirit, fill the hearts of Thy faithful ..." He comes to all where grace abounds — so teaches our faith — and transforms, enlightens, strengthens.

We have our good reasons then, on this occasion which marks both an end and a beginning, for so turning the attention of our minds and the prayer of our hearts to the Holy Spirit by offering this Mass whose prayers and readings center about Him. Thus we recall and commemorate and celebrate the friendship of which He is the author and which is His gift. We remind ourselves that it is in this most intimate and unshakeable and reliable of friendships that we can and must place our hopes. It is fitting then that we turn to Him again today and pray that He come, and being come, remain, the friend rich and generous, constant and never failing.

[12]Jn 15:15.

56

MASS OF PENTECOST

(BACCALAUREATE)

(Acts 2:1–11; 1 Corinthians 12:3–7, 12–13; John 20:19–23)

Your Excellency, Reverend Fathers, graduates, members of the faculty, parents, relatives and friends of the graduates:

We have come here to this campus this morning, from near or from far as the case may be, to share with our graduates the joy of accomplishment which this day is rightfully theirs. They have persevered; they have laid the specter of the senior thesis and will soon receive from the hands of His Excellency proof positive and legal that they have here successfully completed a course of collegiate studies and are entitled to their place in the community of scholars.

We are now absorbed in an indispensable act of the graduation ceremonies and, in fact, the part of greatest efficacy. We are here about this altar united in spirit to offer this Mass. With the graduates and for their intentions we offer again the sacrifice of Calvary, the worship of our Catholic religion. There is no way more fitting to render to Almighty God our thanks for the graces of these last four years; there is no way more efficacious to beg of the Lord His light and support for these young men and women in whatever new and quite different life may now lay open before them.

They need at this particular moment no special exhortation to persevere in the good. Over these years they have taken seriously the Holy Scriptures and studied them as the Word of God; they have had the opportunity to make the acquaintance of St. Augustine, John Damascene, and Anselm; Plato, Aristotle, and St. Thomas. A glimpse of the truth has been accorded them. What they have seen of that truth and made part and parcel of their own convictions is itself its own manner of exhortation, and exhortation of the deepest and most enduring sort; there is here and now no need to attempt any addition thereto.

Today, for the fourth time, the Mass deemed appropriate for our graduation is the Votive Mass of the Holy Spirit, which is in fact the Mass of Pentecost Sunday.

It is never out of season, of course, to turn our attention to God the Holy Spirit, the giver of life, as we refer to Him in the Creed, and implore His light and aid. With good reason, too, we associate the Spirit of Truth with Christian intellectual endeavor, for "He will remind you of all things that I have taught you," was Our Savior's promise to His Apostles,[1] and among the Spirit's gifts are wisdom and understanding, knowledge and counsel. But the Pentecost liturgy suits the event in another way too. Graduation ranks high among the memorable events of life; especially memorable as well is the message of this particular Mass.

To me, and perhaps to the graduates also, the readings of this Pentecost liturgy recall what may have been the summit of the theology course it was my privilege to study with them over this past year. In the closing classes of the first semester, we turned our attention to the names of the Holy Spirit which are "love" and "gift," and to the missions of the Divine Persons. The truths we then considered are among the most deeply moving of our Catholic faith, and we find them recalled here, at least implicitly, in the Pentecost Mass.

The lessons we read just a few moments ago, especially the first and the third, are accounts of events of significance in the Church's earliest days. But more than that, they remind us of truths distinctive of our Catholic faith — its own proper riches, so to speak, and among the most moving thereof — the reality, namely, of the supernatural in our lives, the wonders that God graciously and gratuitously works in the souls of men.

There seems to be in the sanctuaries these days a conspiracy of silence against such truths, thoroughly Catholic though they are, for we hear but little about God's astonishing gifts to us, what He works in us and for us. But the readings of this Pentecost Mass make it abundantly

---

[1] Jn 14:26.

clear that God does not leave the souls of His own to their merely human resources, but reaches within, so to speak, and transfigures them to His own image and a share in His own divine life.

The reading from the Acts of the Apostles recounts the familiar history of the first Pentecost Sunday when the tiny group that was the seed of the Church was gathered in Jerusalem. There was the sound of the wind, first, that filled the house, then the appearance of tongues, as it were, of fire on the heads of each.

But it was in the world of the invisible that the greatest wonders were wrought. If the Spirit was present in the wind and fire as in visible signs, He was present, too, in a way invisible, but nonetheless real, in the minds and hearts of the disciples, and a remarkable transformation His presence wrought — from mute, men became eloquent; from ignorant, wise; from timid, courageous.

The Gospel narrative recalls another mission of the Holy Spirit some weeks previous to the first, on Easter Sunday in fact, to the disciples gathered in the Cenacle room. The risen Christ stood suddenly in their midst though the doors were locked. "Peace to you," was His greeting. He breathed on them and said, "Receive ye the Holy Spirit. Whose sins you shall forgive, they are forgiven them." The Spirit takes up His abode in a special way in Christ's priests, and immediately a share of divine authority is theirs — and the power to forgive sins resides in the Church.

St. Paul in his first letter to the Corinthians, from which the second reading is taken, is abundantly clear that the Spirit limits not His gracious work to apostles and priests. Rather, His grace and gifts He shares with all who will. If anyone can say "Jesus is Lord," believing what he proclaims, this itself is a sign of the presence of the Holy Spirit transforming the soul. "It was in one Spirit that all of us were baptized into one body … All of us have been given to drink of the same Spirit."

And to the Romans he writes of the "charity of God that is poured forth into our hearts by the Holy Spirit."[2] But God is not content with the union of love, for we have Our Savior's solemn affirmation that God Himself in a special way dwells in the souls of those to whom it is given to love Him. "If any man loves me, he will keep my commandments, and

---

[2] Rom 5:5.

my Father will love him, and I will love him, and we will come to him and take up our abode in him."[3]

It begins with grace, this life of the soul that is the gift of the Spirit. Where grace is, God is present in the soul; there is friendship of God and man, and all that friendship entails — willingness to forgive and sharing of gifts. Grace means already a beginning on earth of eternal life.

During our theology class this past year, we turned our attention to several other truths of our faith — to the Mystical Body, for example; to the passion of Christ; and to the sacraments. But we found that all these point to the Pentecost truth and in this find their fulfillment. To be part of the Mystical Body, for instance, is to share in that life of grace that is the Spirit's grace; it was that we might possess this divine life that the Word became Incarnate, suffered, and died. It is, again, that this same life of the Spirit may begin, reach maturity, be nourished, be recovered when lost, strengthened when weak, that Our Savior instituted the sacraments and left them to us. It was our privilege at the end of the year to study the Holy Eucharist, but it is that this same life of the Spirit be nourished that Our Savior left Himself to us in this most blessed of sacraments.

It is a rich Mass then, this Pentecost Mass, richer in Catholic truth than a mere cursory reading might reveal. It reminds us of our true dignity as adoptive sons of God and temples of the Holy Spirit. To the graduates it recalls, now at the end, their most precious possession, at the same time the source of their strength and their hope.

[3] cf. Jn 14:21, 23.

SUMMER FEASTS

57

SAINTS PETER AND PAUL

My dear friends, this day, June 29, in the liturgical calendar of the Church is the day set aside to commemorate the martyrdoms of Saints Peter and Paul and to pay homage to these two giants whom, rightly, we think of as foundation stones of Christ's Church.

The names of these two have been so long linked in Christian memory that we tend to overlook how different these men were. The contrast between them shows at almost every point, but it is a contrast that is both distinctive and consoling. Christ, Our Lord, head of the Body that is the Church, does not flatten out the human personalities of His chosen instruments. He uses men as they are temperamentally.

We look at Peter and Paul, and what first jumps to the eye is the immense difference in their intellectual attainments. Peter is a fisherman from rustic Galilee, and we have no reason to suppose that he enjoyed — or even endured — any particular schooling. We read in the Acts of the Apostles that when Peter and John were arrested in Jerusalem and Peter addressed the lordly Sanhedrin, the members of that august court were astonished at the assurance shown by Peter and John, considering they were uneducated laymen. Paul was born into Roman citizenship in sophisticated, cosmopolitan Tarsus. He studied with the rabbis and was evidently a pretty good student, a part-time theologian who was trained by a celebrated intellectual. "I studied under Gamaliel," he wrote later, "and was taught the exact observance of the law of our ancestors."[1] To the Galatians, Paul says, "You must have heard ... how I stood

[1] Acts 22:3.

out among other Jews of my generation and how I was for the tradition of my ancestors."[2]

There could hardly be a more striking contrast than that between the homespun letters of Peter and the soaring, complex epistles of Paul. No one knew this better than our first Pope himself. With honesty and humility he writes: "Our brother Paul, who is so dear to us ... wrote to you with the wisdom that is his special gift. He always writes like this when he deals with this sort of subject, and this makes some points in his letter hard to understand."[3]

What is most striking is the totally opposite ways in which these two came to the faith of Christ. Slowly, gradually, by laborious trial and error Peter arrives at that splendid confession of which we read in St. Matthew's Gospel. "Who do men say that I am?" "Thou art the Christ, the Son of the living God."[4] Paul, on the contrary, was flattened on the highway by a violent act of the Lord Christ. At the time, he was bent upon an errand of spleen and mischief — persecuting the Christians at Damascus. He was blinded in preparation for receiving that light which is the light of faith. One can find no fault with the pedagogical methods of the Lord Christ; He reaches different people differently. He speaks one way to Nicodemus, the doctor of the law, another to a wide-eyed, light headed woman at Jacob's well. Where strong methods are needed, as with the fiery enthusiast from Tarsus — Paul — the Lord will use them.

The apostolates of the two saints were identical in aim and objective but entirely different in scope. "I had been commissioned to preach the good news to the Gentiles," writes Paul, "just as Peter had been commissioned to preach it to the Jews."[5] So he journeyed to Philippi in Macedonia, and to Corinth and Athens in Greece, and even as far west as Rome.

We may attend to one similarity between the fisherman and the scholar. Both were sinners. Peter denied Christ, Paul persecuted Him. Both repented. Both were forgiven. Both were used for Christ's high purposes. Both responded with humble confidence, and both responded magnificently. Both persevered even to violent death — Peter on the cross, Paul by the stroke of a sword.

---

[2]Gal 1:13–14.   [3]2 Pet 3:15–16.   [4]Mt 16:13, 16.   [5]Gal 2:7.

The prayer of the Mass for this day, the prayer of their feast is — as rightly it should be — a prayer for fidelity. "O God," we pray, "grant that your Church, who first received the teachings of Christ from these two, may always remain faithful to the truths that they taught."

58

SAINT IGNATIUS

In these days we can't help but notice a trend in the liturgy of the Church to accord to the saints lesser and lesser prominence. Perhaps the day is approaching when mention of them will disappear altogether. But the fact still remains that no amount of abstract motivation can attract and inspire us to a closer following of Christ as can the example of one great human being in whom all that is lofty and noble is manifest to us in a concrete and human way. At this Mass, to which we have added a little solemnity, we honor and commemorate such a person — Ignatius of Loyola — most admirable in his union with God, a mirror of Christ in his personality, bordering on the awesome in his accomplishments for the Church of Christ on earth.

The skirmish between the French and the Basques at Pamplona in May of 1521 scarcely merits mention in history texts. Yet it was actually one of the more decisive battles in the history of Christendom. For the cannonball that there shattered the right leg of Inigo de Loyola marked the beginning of a spiritual transformation that, in the providence of God and with the help of His grace, terminated in time in the formation of a heroic lover of Christ and a courageous prudent leader of men united to do for the Church on earth whatever most needed doing at the time.

Beginning with the years of his agonizing recuperation and continuing through the ensuing decade, there was vouchsafed to him, in the providence of God, a clear and moving vision of the Lord Christ. Through Ignatius' own reading and reflection, prayer and meditation,

Father McGovern preached this sermon at Canisius College in New York.

Christ did indeed come through to him, appeared to his mind and heart, and awakened in him a passion of love and loyalty. In him, Mary and Martha were one; while remaining all his life a profound contemplative, he became also a most ardent apostle.

This vision of Christ — Christ, savior of souls; Christ suffering for sin; Christ, teacher of truth; Christ poor; Christ gentle to the afflicted — this vision in time Ignatius distilled into the constitutions of a religious order dedicated to the same cause for which Christ Himself became man, lived, and died, dedicated to the same means for the attainment of that end. This same vision he shared with other strong men. They too were caught by it. His first few companions grew into that "new army" which, in the Collect prayer of today's Mass, we ascribe to the providence of God through the instrumentality of Ignatius Loyola.

The Society of Jesus initially numbered six men. At the time of his death some sixteen years later, St. Ignatius was superior general of some two thousand Jesuits. Through these his sons, his influence made itself felt from the Council halls of Trent to India and Japan. Canisius and Xavier, Faber and Bellarmine, later Jogues and Brebeuf and Regis and Bobola, to mention but a few — these are names to be reckoned with in the history of the Church. Spiritually they were his sons, and from him came their inspiration.

The days of St. Ignatius and the early Jesuits were a time of bitter, sometimes even bloody, division that rent Christian Europe. The first sons of Ignatius labored mightily, and with no small success, to save Europe for the Church and from the ravages of the Reformation. In the eyes of Ignatius, the Church of Rome was Christ Himself continuing His salvific work on earth, Christ teaching through His vicar, the Bishop of Rome. Love of Christ was inseparable from love of the Church, loyalty to Christ unthinkable apart from loyalty to His vicar through whom Christ continues to speak. This message rings out loud and clear, like a bell, in the constitutions of his Society. It rings out just as loud and clear in his *Spiritual Exercises*, that unemotional little book that has set so many hearts on fire and filled the history of the Church with heroes.

Today we are gathered in the chapel of a school founded by

latter-day sons of Ignatius for the same purpose for which he founded his Society. This school is named for one of his closest friends and most loyal disciples. And so it is fitting that here today we honor the memory of Ignatius Loyola. We beg his intercession on our behalf. It is also appropriate that during these times which are like his, though to a lesser degree, times of division and dissension in the Church, we hearken to this message of his, this appeal for loyalty to Christ's Church.

59

ASSUMPTION

(Luke 1:39–56)

"He who is mighty has done great things for me" were Mary's words to her cousin Elizabeth, as we read just a few moments ago. Today the entire Church on earth joins with the angels and saints in heaven in rejoicing with the Blessed Mother of God because of one of these great things that the Almighty has done for her: that privilege, namely, that we contemplate in the fourth glorious mystery of the Rosary and to which we refer as her assumption into heaven.

It was only twenty-nine years ago, on November 1, 1950, that Pope Pius XII defined that Mary's assumption is contained in the deposit of Christian faith: "We pronounce, declare, and define it to be a divinely revealed dogma that the Immaculate Mother of God, the ever-Virgin Mary, having completed the course of her earthly life, was assumed body and soul into heavenly glory."[1]

It is by no means the point of the dogma that the Blessed Mother of Christ did not die. In fact Pope Pius in the course of the apostolic constitution makes some seven or eight references to her death. The feast of the Assumption existed in the Church from time immemorial. His Holiness comments on this feast and informs us that its lesson is "not only that the dead body of the Blessed Virgin Mary remained incorrupt, but that she gained a triumph out of death, her heavenly glorification after the example of her only-begotten Son, Jesus Christ."

We have to judge it right that the Blessed Mother of God so share in the glory of her Son's resurrection. "The Scriptures," proclaimed Pope

---

[1] Apostolic Constitution on the Dogma of the Assumption, *Munificentissimus Deus*, 44.

Pius, "set the revered Mother of God before our eyes as most intimately joined to her Divine Son and as always sharing His lot."

God Himself is, of course, the cause of that supernatural reality that we call grace that transfigures the created, spiritual substance into the likeness of the Divinity Himself. St. Thomas points out on more occasions than one that just as that body which is closest to the fire participates the most in the heat thereof, so in proportion to a creature's proximity to God is that creature's fullness of grace.

And so the soul of Christ, united to God in the unity of a single Person, is filled with grace with a fullness beyond that of any other creature; the only limit, in fact, to that fullness is on the part of grace itself. The angels, pure spirits that they are, are closer to God in nature than we; as His ministering spirits they are closer in function and familiarity; hence they are by far our superiors in grace, like the light of the sun to a spark. To signify this, appearances of the angels in the Scripture are generally accompanied by light. But no angel was so close to God as to be His mother. As St. Thomas expressed it, "The Blessed Virgin Mary was closest to Christ with respect to humanity because from her He received His human nature. And therefore she must have received from Christ the fullness of grace above all others."[2]

On any number of occasions in Old Testament times, an angel was sent to this man or that with a message or directions from on high. In each and every instance, it was the human who greeted the angel, the human who deferred, who showed the reverence — until Gabriel was sent to Mary of Nazareth. For the first time then, it was the angel who showed reverence, the angel who recognized his superior, and in the words of Gabriel's greeting is contained the reason for his deference: "Hail, full of grace."[3]

We catch a glimpse here of the wonders that grace can accomplish. It can elevate a mere human soul to a dignity and nobility above the nine choirs of ministering spirits: "Queen of Angels" we salute her in the litany, and with good reason.

Such godliness, in turn, means sinlessness, as befits her who is to be mother of Christ who conquered sin. She alone, of all Adam's sons and

---

[2]*Summa Theologiae*, IIIa, q. 27, a. 5.   [3]Lk 1:28.

daughters, never had the occasion to say on her own behalf a Confiteor, or an Act of Contrition. Godliness such as hers means perfection of human manners. In her, God's idea of what a human being can be did not perish. She is the mother most amiable and the mother most admirable, and in the entire history of our race she stands as the one perfect lady.

Death came into this world in punishment for sin. It makes no sense that the sinless mother of Christ should have suffered the indignities consequent upon death.

We rejoice with her today and are grateful that at least one of our race has so found favor with God and risen to such heights of loveable and attractive holiness. We have reason to rejoice for ourselves, too, because her present glorious existence is a token and a radiant pledge of what lies in store for the person of faith. Body and soul united in heaven — this, too, is to be our ultimate state. The robe of glory which she now wears is meant to be ours ultimately as well. God helping, Mary interceding, let us shape ourselves to it.

THIS MOST BLESSED OF SACRAMENTS

We are here this morning to direct our thoughts to the Holy Eucharist, to reconsider — as we cannot too often do — just what this sacrament is according to the teachings of the Church, its magnitude and its overwhelming grandeur. As Pope John Paul II named it, the *Inaestimabile Donum* — the inestimable gift.

St. Luke, in his account of the Last Supper, reports that Our Lord Jesus Christ, when He opened His final discourse to His chosen twelve at the end of that repast, began with the words, "With longing have I longed to eat this Pasch with you."[1] Words these are which must have aroused a certain wonder in the minds of His Apostles when they heard them. What was to occur at this repast that was to render it so special, in such an extraordinary way an object of longing on the part of their Lord and Master?

They had not so long to wait. Shortly, having offered for the last time the Paschal lamb as a sacrifice pleasing to God, the Lord Christ offered for the first time the sacrifice of the New Law. He took the bread into His hands, as St. Luke relates, and said the words of consecration: "This is my body," and then the chalice of wine, "This is the new testament in my blood." He said this with His instructions, "Do this in memory of me."[2]

With these words He gave to His disciples, and through them to theirs, and to ourselves in time, the gift precious beyond the power of any Apostle, or ourselves, or of any man, to suspect, imagine, or

[1]Lk 22:15. [2]Lk 22:19-20.

210

desire — the gift of His own human and Divine self as food for our spiritual lives.

Human life needs nourishment. In a parallel way, so too does the life of the soul. Bread and wine are food and drink, and through these — as signs — the Lord Christ has given us His body and blood as just such food. Their mode of nourishing is just the opposite of that of natural food. The food we eat is transformed into us, and so nourishes and sustains us. But the supernatural food of the soul, which is Christ, operates in just the opposite fashion. Christ is not transformed into us, but rather transforms us into Him, rooting and establishing us the more deeply and firmly in that Mystical Body of His which is His Church. This the sacrament does through the grace and charity that it brings, through which we are the more able to love the Lord our God with our whole heart and with our whole soul and with our whole mind, and our neighbor as ourselves for the love of God.

By means of this sacrament, from the time of His birth in Bethlehem until the world's end, Christ's followers might be never without Him. He was with His Apostles; He is still with us, only in a different mode.

As Pope Paul VI notes in his encyclical of September 1965, *Mysterium Fidei*, by so deigning to remain with us, the Lord Christ bestows an incomparable dignity upon the Christian people. As His Holiness expresses it:

> While the Eucharist is reserved in churches and oratories, Christ is truly Emmanuel, which means, "God with us." He, the Incarnate God, is with us day and night. He dwells among us with the fullness of grace and truth; He raises the level of morals, fosters virtue, comforts the sorrowing, and stirs up all those who draw near to Him to imitate Him.

This encyclical to which I have just alluded is, in fact, the last document of a doctrinal nature and of any length issued by the Holy See on the subject of the Eucharist. Its title is *Mysterium Fidei*, the Mystery of Faith, an epithet that has, in the Church, always been reserved for the Holy Eucharist.

If we understand by the word "mystery," in the context, a truth of our Faith that we cannot understand but assent to nonetheless on the authority of God revealing, then indeed the deposit of our Catholic Faith abounds in mysteries. The Trinity is such, certainly: How this can be — three Persons in one God — must always elude our understanding this side of heaven's very special light. Moreover, the Trinity assumes a certain logical priority over the other mysteries. Belief in God the Son, for instance, is presupposed to belief in the Incarnation and thus to all the other mysteries pertaining to Christ. Yet, nonetheless, it is the Holy Eucharist, and not the Trinity, nor any other mystery, to which the Church has always assigned the title "Mystery of Faith."

With the help of God's good grace, we assent to the mystery of the Trinity and so assent to a truth we cannot understand. But in regard to the Eucharist, we freely and gladly assent not only to a truth we cannot understand, but even to the contrary of what our senses tell us. What strikes our eyes, our taste, our sense of touch, tells us that this particle is bread; the word of Christ affirms "No, this is my body." As St. Thomas Aquinas writes in his hymn, *Adoro Te Devote*:

> Sight, taste, and touch are in Thee deceived;
> The ear alone most safely is believed.
> I believe all the Son of God has spoken,
> Than Truth's own word there is no truer spoken.

Belief in the Eucharist, in other words, makes greater demands on our faith than does any other mystery. Perhaps it is for this reason that it is named "Mystery of Faith."

There are, perhaps, other reasons, too, for this same fact. Perhaps it is the mystery of faith because it is so central to the practice of our faith, the mystery about which the exercise of our faith revolves. From the point of view of Christian worship, what would we do without it?

What holocausts, sin offerings, and peace offerings were, by Divine command, to the Chosen People of the Old Testament time, the Mass is for us. For the Mass, which consists essentially in the separate consecrations of the bread and wine, is our sacrifice. As Pope Paul VI expresses it, "What was carried out on Calvary is re-enacted in wonderful fashion and is constantly recalled, and its saving power is applied to forgiving us the sins we commit each day."

Moreover, wherever the Eucharist is, there is the center of our spiritual life.

In itself, indeed, the Eucharist is a sign of Christian unity. For the wafer of bread is one wafer from many grains, and the cup of wine is pressed from many grapes. Each is in that way symbolic of Christ's Mystical Body, one Body of many members, and of this Body we are a part.

But the Eucharist does not stop with being a sign. As is true of all the sacraments, what it signifies, that it brings about. By the grace which is its effect, by the charity it fosters through the power of God, this sacrament does indeed unify ever and ever more closely those members of Christ's Mystical Body who are faithful to its devout and worthy reception.

There are, as we know from our grammar school days, seven sacraments belonging to the Church of Christ, bequeathed to her by her founder Himself. Each of them is a sign by which He sanctifies the souls of His followers. Insofar as all the sacraments so sanctify in this Church of Christ, all are, indeed, blessed.

Yet this title — Blessed Sacrament — we reserve for one sacrament and one only. The Eucharist is indeed pre-eminent over all the others, and enjoys the highest place in their hierarchy. Christ works through all the others; this one, actually, substantially contains that same Christ Himself who works through all the others.

All the other sacraments we treat with respect and reverence; this one we actually worship as God. For indeed it is Christ who is God under the appearances of bread and wine. Because we hold this with the unshakable certitude of faith, we genuflect to the Host, treat every particle of every Host with greatest respect, and direct our attention, our requests, our needs, our acts of contrition for our sins, to Him who is contained therein.

We had occasion to mention earlier that the encyclical of Pope

Paul VI was entitled *Mysterium Fidei*, and we offered a reason or two why this title has been, and is, reserved for the Eucharist.

Actually, in the last couple of decades the phrase "*mysterium fidei*" has had a somewhat strange history within the Mass. Many of us who are willing to date ourselves will remember when *mysterium fidei* was part of the form of the consecration of the wine itself: "*Hic est enim calix sanguinis mei, novi et aeterni testamenti:* mysterium fidei: *qui pro vobis et pro multis effundetur in remissionem peccatorum.*" Then sometime after the Second Vatican Council the phrase was removed from the formula and placed after it, to be recited after the genuflection. But then a strange thing happened, at least in the English rendition: it became incorporated into the acclamation, "Let us proclaim the mystery of faith." And then some acclamation was added, such as "Christ is risen" or one of the others, and the net impression of it all is that it is what follows the proclamation that is the mystery of faith, and not the Holy Eucharist whose consecration has just preceded and which always has been regarded as the mystery of faith.

Encyclicals have a way of being occasioned by budding heterodoxy, and Pope Paul's *Mysterium Fidei* is no exception. The Holy Father speaks in this document of a doctrine appearing, spreading, which teaches in essence that the consecrated bread and consecrated wine are no more than a symbol of Christ's spiritual and guiding presence in His Church — the kind of presence He spoke of one time when He said: "For where there are two or three gathered in my name, there am I in the midst of them."[3]

In the face of this, Pope Paul reaffirms what has been the "constant teaching that the Church has always passed on to catechumens, and what the words that Christ used when He instituted the Holy Eucharist all require us to believe, namely that the Eucharist is the flesh of Our Savior Jesus Christ which suffered for our sins and which the Father in His loving kindness raised again."

Pope Paul, then, insists on affirming the Catholic doctrine as it has always been since the earliest Doctors of the Church first considered seriously what the Eucharist is, and as it was taught to you and me. In

[3]Mt 18:20.

affirming the doctrine, he used a noun familiar to you and me, but most likely not to your children — transubstantiation. In *Mysterium Fidei*, His Holiness insists on this as exactly the right and fitting word to signify what the power of God effects at the consecration of the Mass: in the words of Pope Paul, "a marvelous conversion of the bread into the body and the whole substance of the wine into the blood of Christ." Through the words of consecration, the Pope insists, "Christ is really present, whole and entire, God and man," and "of the bread and wine nothing remains but the appearances."

In his encyclical, Pope Paul VI has occasion to allude to the liturgical changes then — in 1965 — about to be instituted under the inspiration of the Second Vatican Council. He expresses their goal, the purpose of great good he hopes will be achieved by them:

> We earnestly hope that the restoration of the Sacred Liturgy will provide abundant fruits in the form of Eucharistic devotion so that the Holy Church may, with this salvific sign of piety raised on high, make daily progress toward the full achievement of unity, inviting all Christians to a unity of faith and love, and drawing them to it gently, through the action of divine grace.

Now, nineteen years later, we reflect on the changes that have been introduced and on the status of the Blessed Sacrament as it is regarded in the Church today, and we might just wonder about the extent to which Pope Paul's hopes have been realized. If anything, it seems that the Holy Eucharist is now less a "salvific sign of piety raised on high" than it was then, for the Blessed Sacrament — externally, at least — in the light of the various liturgical practices of the Church today is less revered than then, less respected than then, now less than then a mystery of faith uniting Catholics in one bond of belief and worship.

The various changes that have been introduced since the Second Vatican Council have been, taken singly, small ones indeed, and concerned with the accidental, not the essential. For each, as it has been introduced, sufficient reason has always been advanced. Yet taking these changes cumulatively, it seems that their net effect has been a gradual lessening of the reverence — in fact, of the proper sort of adoration — owed this august sacrament, owed indeed to God Himself, sacramentally present among us.

There have been many such changes, and we are all familiar with all of them. For the most part, each change has been in the direction of less reverence. As instances of what I mean: It is no longer the Eucharist, as we mentioned before, that is dignified in the Mass by the title "Mystery of Faith," but some other aspect of our redemption. The words of consecration are no longer given the central place they once were given by being printed in letters extra large on the page of the priest's missal. People now generally receive Communion standing, although kneeling is the more reverent posture, the posture appropriate to adoration. In many churches, the Blessed Sacrament is no longer in its place of honor in the center of the sanctuary but has been pushed back into the wings. Altars tend to be plain now, no longer things of beauty appropriate to the august sacrifice that is offered upon them.

Time there was when such reverence was manifested toward the Sacred Host and the contents of the chalice that only the consecrated hands of the priest touched such things. Modern catechisms, if they treat the Real Presence at all, pay it but little heed. Lastly, people now — as it is an approved thing to do — receive the consecrated Hosts in their hands, thus treating them as they treat any other bread. Even the remission of the regulations regarding fasting, blessing though it is in many respects, tends to diminish the awe in which we ought to stand in the presence of this sacrament.

True enough, Catholic people receive Communion in large numbers. But on the other hand, the number of confessions has markedly diminished in recent years. In the face of this, we are led to wonder whether that same concern still reigns in the hearts of the people to assure, as well as they can, that their souls are properly adorned for the Holy One whom they are about to receive.

The changes, taken cumulatively, seem to generate the impression that in the Sacred Host and the consecrated wine, there is not all that much to be venerated.

In the face of this, it would then be a good thing to do just what we have been doing here: recalling the truths of our Catholic Faith concerning the Eucharist and the inestimable grandeur and magnitude of the gift. These truths have remained ever unchanged. In the light then of this reawakened understanding, let us see to it that, with the help of God's grace, the dispositions of our soul — humility, reverence, adoration, gratitude, love — may be always what they ought to be toward this most blessed of sacraments.

AFTERWORD

With great delight I sat in his shadow,
And his fruit was sweet to my taste.
　　　　　　— Canticle of Canticles 2:3

At Thomas Aquinas College the classes are run as discussions, and students are divided into "sections," which are groups of about seventeen students who have all their classes, except the evening seminar, together. In the fall of 1984 I was a sophomore at the college, as was my future husband, Tony Andres. That year we sophomores had the distinction of being divided into what felt like — perhaps were — the two worst sections ever. In one section went the majority of the talkers, in another the majority of the quiet students. Classes were a crucifixion … except for philosophy class which, led by Father McGovern, was an amazing experience for all of us, and my favorite class of the four-year curriculum.

Father Thomas Aquinas McGovern was a wonderful teacher and priest, and his death that spring came as a shock to students and faculty alike. He had been heard to say that God should take him instead of fellow tutor Norman DeSilva who was dying of a brain tumor. Norman was a young man with a wife and family, and Father felt that an old Jesuit like himself would be less of a loss to the community. Never one for half measures, God took them both. Father died February 19, 1985, and Norman outlived him only until July 1.

Father McGovern left behind what amounted to three thick binders full of manually typed sermons. While we were still students, Dr. McArthur set his assistant Tricia Lemmon to work organizing them, and she in turn assigned my classmate and friend Maria Reinagel to help.

Consequently, when our graduation came in the spring of 1987, I had the perfect present for Tony: three fat red binders full of the photocopied sermons of Father Thomas Aquinas McGovern. After we married, we moved those three binders no less than nine times as we made our way from Indiana to Virginia and eventually back to Thomas Aquinas College.

My labor of love in carting the collected sermons around was nothing compared to Father's toil in writing and delivering them. Reliable sources tell me it took him about nine hours to prepare each sermon. He would type it out, then revise — my copies show frequent pencil corrections on the final draft: a more felicitous phrase here, a more concise expression there. He then memorized each sermon. Although he always brought his typed pages to the lectern, he never looked at them.

Beginning with Brendan Kelly (not yet ordained) as a graduate student at Notre Dame in the fall of 1987, and ending with Father Brendan Kelly (priest for the Diocese of Lincoln) visiting Dr. McArthur in the fall of 2013, there was talk of publishing some of the sermons. That I now have the privilege of seeing this project through to its completion came about as follows:

In August 2010, I bought an old IBM electric typewriter. To make good use of it I started typing out Father McGovern's sermons. Granted, turning photocopies of manually typed sermons into a set of electrically typed sermons does not seem like a huge step forward toward publication … but God's ways, while not always seeming the most efficient, are always the most effective.

The death of founder and tutor Marcus Berquist on All Souls Day of that year, combined with the beauty of the sermons I was typing, led me to approach Dr. McArthur with the suggestion (not a new one) to finally publish a selection. Dr. McArthur was enthusiastic as ever, and that Christmas he answered editorial questions and proofed a beginning set of sermons for me.

Fast forward to the fall of 2013. Father Brendan came out to California for the wedding of his niece and thus, providentially, was able to visit the now ailing Dr. McArthur. Father Brendan and Dr. McArthur discussed Father McGovern's sermons, and both of them reminded me of my task — to prepare the sermons for publication. That the sermons had not yet been published, that I had been distracted by other projects and amusements, I submit as proof of Father McGovern's profound humility, which had yet to be overcome by Dr. McArthur's loving admiration. I told Dr. and Mrs. McArthur, their dear friend Cathy Walsh (an alumna of the College) and my husband that I would get back to work.

On a particularly joy-filled visit to Dr. McArthur about two weeks later, I talked with him and Mrs. McArthur and Cathy again about the sermons, and as Cathy left the room to retrieve a book she said, "Ask Ron to write the Foreword."

"Of course," I replied.

"Ask him now," she persisted.

"Okay," I said. "Dr. McArthur, will you write the Foreword to the book?"

"Sure," he said from his rocking chair, "I'll do that."

After a moment though, in typical Dr. McArthur fashion he said, "You could get someone better, you know."

"Yes," I said, "I know, but we want you to do it."

"Okay," he said, "I'll do it."

That was on Thursday, October 10, 2013. The following Tuesday the McArthurs sent out an email asking for prayers for a holy death: Dr. McArthur was in the final stages of renal disease. He died two days later on Thursday, October 17, the feast of St. Margaret Mary.

As I thought back on our visits, one thing didn't make sense. Why had Cathy, knowing he was near death, told me to ask him for the Foreword? All along I'd been planning to do so, but knowing he was dying, wouldn't Cathy have known he didn't have the time or energy?

A few days after the funeral, Cathy answered my questions with a sheaf of paper. She'd had me ask him because it was something she knew he'd want to do, and something he wouldn't have done on his own. He would have waited for me to ask. So knowing we didn't have much time left, she told me to ask. He said yes, and that sheaf of papers was the Foreword.

Tricia Lemmon, devoted friend and assistant to the end, had prompted and taken dictation from him on Saturday, October 12. On Monday, October 14, Dr. McArthur had breakfast, the last meal he ate. On Tuesday, October 15, two days before he died, Dr. McArthur dictated to Tricia the concluding paragraphs of the Foreword, on the sermons themselves. It was the last work he did.

The Sermons

The sermons in this volume comprise roughly one-quarter of Father McGovern's sermons. I have included 60; Father left us 236.

Of the sermons for the seasons of the liturgical year, those I have left out are nearly all additional sermons for the Sundays and feasts already included. Of the sermons for various feasts and occasions, those excluded were, again, additional sermons for feasts and occasions already represented.

Left out altogether are more than 100 sermons for the Sundays through the year, which sermons are nearly equally divided among the A, B, and C cycles of readings. A selection of these sermons may comprise a companion volume at a later date.

Dr. McArthur and Father McGovern loved to play tennis together — although Dr. McArthur complained that Father was so diligent he often turned down an invitation because he had a sermon or class to prepare. I like to think of them now: enjoying the Beatific Vision, still the best of friends. With the publication of these sermons nearly thirty years after the death of Father McGovern, Dr. McArthur's persistent loving admiration has finally conquered his friend's profound humility, as love always conquers in the end. May the teaching of St. Thomas, to which both of these men were devoted, shine forth from these pages and light our way until we join them in glory.

Suzie Andres
Santa Paula
September 8, 2014
Nativity of Our Lady

BIOGRAPHICAL NOTE

Thomas Aquinas McGovern was born on May 18, 1921, in the Bronx, New York, to Thomas and Mary (Rutledge) McGovern. He was the oldest of five children, his siblings being Margaret Mary, Rose Marie, Robert, and John. Thomas attended elementary school at Our Lady Queen of Martyrs in Forest Hills, New York, and went to high school on a full scholarship at Bishop Loughlin in Brooklyn.

On September 7, 1938, at the age of seventeen, Thomas entered the Society of Jesus. He obtained his Bachelor of Arts in 1944 from Weston College in Weston, Massachusetts, and his Master of Arts in 1948 from Fordham University.

On June 17, 1951, when he was thirty years old, Thomas was ordained a priest for the Society of Jesus.

Father Thomas McGovern was awarded his Licentiate in Sacred Theology one year later, in 1952, at Woodstock College in Woodstock, Maryland. He went on to study at Université Laval in Quebec City and received his Doctorate of Philosophy in 1957.

For sixteen years, from 1956 to 1972, Father McGovern was an associate professor of philosophy at Canisius College in Buffalo, New York.

In early 1972, at fifty-one years of age, Father Thomas Aquinas McGovern joined the faculty of Thomas Aquinas College, then in Calabasas, California. He taught across the curriculum: mathematics, natural science, language (including an advanced Latin class), music, seminar, philosophy, and theology. In 1976 he was elected to the Board of Governors and served as a governor until his death.

Father McGovern was an avid, competitive (but humble) tennis and racquetball player and a powerful swimmer. As a young man he would often be "waved" back in toward shore by lifeguards at Far Rockaway beach when he unknowingly swam too far out, too quickly, into the ocean. In later years, as a priest and a host, he enjoyed treating the competition to a whiskey sour after a hard-fought game of racquetball.

Once he had made the move to Thomas Aquinas College, Father returned yearly to Canisius to teach summer school. Driving his light blue VW station wagon across the country, he would ferry students to their homes in the East for the vacation, staying in KOAs along the way, and returning, students in tow, for the new school year at summer's end.

Father was a beloved teacher at Canisius as well as at Thomas Aquinas College. When he left Canisius to move to California, his students gave him a copy of the McKeon edition of Aristotle's basic works inscribed to "Stewey," their nickname for him, likely based on a chalkboard character he used (stick-figure style) to illustrate Aristotle's *Physics*.

In his last year of teaching, he enlivened the *Physics* once again for his students at Thomas Aquinas, this time with examples of a dog. After a semester's worth of anecdotes, he finally had cause to write the dog's name on the chalkboard: Phydeaux.

Father Thomas Aquinas McGovern was a tutor at Thomas Aquinas College for thirteen years, until he died from a heart attack on February 19, 1985, three months shy of his sixty-fourth birthday.

The following year he received posthumously the College's highest honor, the Saint Thomas Aquinas Medallion.